The Family Wealth Formula:

The Proven Guide for Money Management, Generational Wealth, And Family Financial Leadership

Anthane C. Richie Sr.

Table of Contents

Introduction

On Tuesday nights in a lot of homes that look like yours, everything is "fine." The mortgage drafts on time. Paychecks land. Retirement contributions happen in the background. The kids get to soccer, orthodontist appointments, and school projects, mostly on schedule. You're doing the things responsible adults are supposed to do. And yet, somewhere between loading the dishwasher and collapsing on the couch, a quiet thought keeps returning: if one big thing went wrong, how much of this holds together? You're not drowning, but you don't feel safe either.

You and your partner probably don't lack information. You've listened to podcasts, watched a bunch of YouTube videos, skimmed articles, maybe even tried a budgeting app. You've heard you should have an emergency fund, maximize your 401(k), use your Health Savings Account (HSA) correctly, pick the "right" health plan, buy enough life and disability coverage, save for college, avoid bad debt, invest for retirement, maybe think about trusts—and do it all while answering work emails and signing school permission slips. What you actually have is not a plan, but a pile of half-implemented tips scattered across logins, statements, and mental notes. No one ever showed you how all the moving parts are supposed to work together for a real family with limited time and attention.

Underneath the surface, there are specific stressors you can probably name if you slow down for a moment. One of you handles most of the money tasks and carries the mental load of "what if?" The other is vaguely aware of the big picture but doesn't know the passwords, the policy details, or where the documents live. You both suspect your insurance coverage is "probably fine," but couldn't say with confidence what would actually happen if a job disappeared, or if one of you couldn't work for six months. You might have three or four retirement accounts from past jobs, a 529 you haven't checked in a year, and a credit card balance that comes and goes but never really feels finished.

On good days, you tell yourselves this is just what modern life is like. On harder days, the questions are sharper. Are we actually okay, or are we one bad diagnosis away from watching everything unravel? If one of us were gone, could the other keep the house and keep the kids' lives relatively stable—or would they be left trying to guess how the finances work while grieving? Are we saving enough for retirement, or are we just hoping future-us is somehow better at this than present-us? Why do money conversations between two competent adults so often turn into tension, silence, or the same argument on repeat?

If any of that sounds familiar, this book is written for you. Not for people who want to spend their weekends optimizing spreadsheets, not for twenty somethings just starting out, and not for ultra wealthy families with full-time advisors on retainer. It's for the couple in their 30s, 40s, or 50s who are in the thick of careers, kids, mortgages, and competing priorities—and who are tired of feeling like they're managing a growing list of financial chores instead of leading a coherent plan together.

You do not need another list of disconnected tips. You need an operating system—a simple structure that tells your money where to go, in what order, and how to protect what you're building. That is what this book will give you: a family wealth operating system that organizes your financial life into four linked layers: foundation, protection, growth, and legacy. The goal is not perfection; the goal is confident leadership. You will move from "I hope this works" to "we know what we're doing, why we're doing it, and how to adjust when life changes."

We start with the foundation: visibility and flow. In the early chapters you'll build a one page family wealth dashboard that shows, at a glance, what you own, what you owe, what it costs to run your household, and where your biggest risks and leaks are. You'll replace vague worry with concrete numbers. You'll then design a cash flow system that doesn't require you to track every latte, but still makes sure essentials, goals, and everyday spending each get what they need—automatically and predictably. This is where overwhelm begins to ease, because you stop running your financial life from memory.

Once you can see clearly, we turn to protection: defending the income and structure your family relies on. You will learn how to right size your emergency fund for real disruptions, not just flat tires. You'll evaluate life and disability insurance in plain language, based on what your household would actually need if one income stopped. You'll put basic estate planning in place—wills, powers of attorney, guardianship decisions, and an emergency binder—so that if something happens, your spouse or co parent is not left in the dark, guessing what you would have wanted while trying to keep the lights on.

With the foundation and protection layers in place, we shift to growth. You'll clarify a practical order of operations for saving, debt payoff, and investing, so you're not constantly wondering whether that extra dollar should go to the mortgage, the 529, or the 401(k). You'll learn how to use tax advantaged accounts intelligently, how to build a simple, durable investment approach without chasing headlines, and how to run a straightforward retirement gap analysis that tells you, in real numbers, what "enough" looks like for your household—and what levers you can pull if there's a shortfall.

From there, we apply the same structure to the decisions that tend to cause the most guilt and confusion. You'll design a college and education funding plan that supports your children without sacrificing your own long term stability. You'll examine housing and real estate choices as strategic levers, not status symbols. You'll think analytically about income growth and side streams so that new dollars actually accelerate your goals instead of being swallowed by lifestyle creep. Throughout, we keep the system grounded in your real constraints: limited hours, unpredictable weeks, and the need to protect your energy as much as your bank accounts.

Finally, we tackle legacy—not as a slogan, but as a set of decisions you can implement. You'll see how to protect your household from lawsuits, property losses, and identity theft. You'll learn how to teach your kids about money in ways that build competence instead of entitlement, using small, repeated experiences long before they handle real sums. We'll explore how to design an inheritance and giving plan that passes on both resources and the mindset to steward them well, so that what you build is not undone within a single generation. The book closes by showing you how to keep the entire system running with an annual reset and a few light touch check ins each year, so you never have to start from scratch again.

This is not a book you need to study for hours at a time. It is a handbook to use alongside your actual life. The most effective way to read it is as a team, in small pieces. For the first month, I suggest you block out two short money sessions per week—20 to 30 minutes each. In one session, you read a section or a chapter. In the other, you implement one concrete step: drafting your dashboard, scheduling an insurance review, setting up a second checking account, or running your first "family wealth review." Each chapter ends with specific actions, checklists, or scripts so you always know what to do next.

If reading together isn't realistic, divide and conquer. One partner can read a chapter and highlight the two or three decisions that matter most; the other can skim those highlights and focus on the checklists and scripts. Use the sample phrases to change how your money conversations start, so discussions that used to spiral into conflict can become shorter, calmer, and more productive. Treat the tools in this book as prototypes—adapt the dashboard, the monthly review, and the priority order to fit your personalities and schedules, rather than trying to copy anything perfectly.

You do not have to become a different kind of person to make this work. You do not need to love spreadsheets or follow financial news. What you do need is a willingness to see your situation clearly, to make a handful of deliberate choices in a sensible order, and to show up with your partner as co leaders instead of opponents. The rest is structure. When the system is simple, the next step is usually obvious and small enough to do after a long day.

The place to begin is not with a product, an app, or a drastic budget. It is with a single page that tells you, honestly, where you are and what your household actually costs to run. In the next chapter, you'll build that one page view and your first monthly rhythm. Before you turn the page, all you need is a rough list of your accounts, your major debts, and last month's bank or credit card statements. Bring those with you. We'll turn "fine, but fragile" into something sturdier—one decision, and one simple system, at a time.

Chapter 1: From Overwhelm to Operating System

On a Tuesday night that looks very much like yours, a family is doing "fine." Both partners work. The kids are shuttled between school, sports, and orthodontist appointments. Retirement contributions come out of paychecks. The mortgage is getting paid. On paper, this is a successful, responsible household.

Yet if you pressed pause, you'd notice something under the surface. One spouse lies awake running numbers, wondering, "If one of us got sick or laid off, how long could we float the mortgage?" The other avoids opening the credit card app because the balance is...roughly fine, they think. Neither is sure how the health insurance deductible works or whether the life insurance through work would really cover everything. They talk about money mostly when there is a problem: a surprise bill, a declined card, an argument about whether a trip is "responsible right now."

This chapter exists for that household. Not because they're careless, but because they are trying to manage a complex financial life with a pile of disconnected tips instead of a simple operating system. When you see money as a string of chores and emergencies, it will always feel fragile. When you see it as part of how you lead your family, protecting each other, planning ahead, and building something durable, your decisions begin to line up and the anxiety starts to drop. Our aim is to replace overwhelm with structure: to show you why "doing many things right" still feels uncertain, and to give you the first building blocks of your family wealth operating system.

Why Smart Families Still Feel Financially Uncertain

If you feel like you should be further ahead by now, you are not alone. Modern families are asked to make unusually complex choices about saving, investing, and risk, often with little training. Research on household finance finds that the cognitive demands of managing investments and long-term planning rank among the highest tasks families face, and that skills like numeracy materially affect how well households build and manage wealth. It's not that you're "bad with money;" the game has become more complex while most of us are playing it on the fly.

Complexity Is the New Risk

Thirty years ago, a typical family might have had one checking account, one savings account, and a pension handled by an employer. Today, even a "simple" household can be juggling two checking accounts, joint savings, multiple credit cards, two 401(k)s, a Health Savings Plan (HSA), a 529, stock options or an Employee Stock Purchase Plan (ESPPs), an online savings account, and a robo-advisor or brokerage account. Add employer benefits, health insurance options, disability plans, Flexible Spending Accounts (FSA), legal plans, and you have a dashboard's worth of decisions, but no dashboard.

Scattered logins and paper statements don't just feel messy; they create blind spots. You might be over-insured in one place and dangerously underinsured in another. You might be paying high fees in an old employer plan while carefully optimizing a small Roth IRA. Benefits choices like selecting a high-deductible health plan without fully funding an HSA, or defaulting into a conservative investment option quietly shape outcomes for years. "Set it and forget it" easily becomes "set it and never check it," comfortable in the moment but hazardous over time. Complexity becomes a form of risk: what you can't see, you can't manage.

The Cost of Unspoken Assumptions

Complexity would be hard enough for one person; most of you are navigating it with a partner who does not think or feel about money the way you do. One of you might see money as security, cash in the bank, a paid-off house, lots of insurance. The other might see money as freedom, experiences, opportunities, education, the ability to change careers. Neither is wrong, but if those scripts stay unspoken, they collide in daily decisions.

Picture a saver who feels calm only when there is six months of expenses in cash, married to a spender who feels suffocated if every purchase is scrutinized. The saver quietly judges the coffees, sports gear, and vacations. The spender quietly resents that money seems to matter more than joy. Or a risk-averse partner who wants most investments in cash or bonds paired with a growth-focused partner who believes in long-term stock investing. Without a shared framework, every market wobble becomes a referendum on who is "right." Silence turns small gaps into big resentments, and money stops being a neutral planning topic and becomes loaded with shame, control, or avoidance. Both partners want safety for the family; without a common plan, they experience each other as obstacles instead of allies.

Protection Gaps Hide in Plain Sight

Another reason responsible families feel fragile is that many big risks are assumed to be handled when they are not. You may know, vaguely, that you have life insurance "through work," but not how much or for how long. You might never have checked who is listed as beneficiary on retirement accounts or group policies. You may not have updated those designations since before marriage or children. Advance directives, powers of attorney, and basic wills sit on a mental to-do list for years.

The risk is concrete. A single income shock, job loss, illness, or disability can force all your careful monthly decisions into a corner. Without adequate life or disability coverage, or with outdated beneficiaries, a disruption can become a crisis: selling investments at the worst possible time, raiding retirement accounts, refinancing on poor terms, or taking on high-interest debt just to cover basics. When families say, "We're one bad event away from everything changing," they are often sensing these invisible protection gaps. My grandma likes to say "You're living one step away from oblivion." The pressure can feel overwhelming but you can change things.

Systems Beat Willpower

Faced with complexity, misalignment, and invisible risk, most people reach for more willpower. “We just need to stick to a budget.” “We should pay more attention.” Relying on willpower alone is like running a business from memory: admirable but unsustainable. Your life is already full; you are not going to become a full-time bookkeeper, nor should you.

What works in research and real households is systems. Instead of asking, “Can I resist overspending this month?” you build a structure where the important things happen automatically and you decide only on the edges. Instead of “We should look at this more often,” you create a simple dashboard and a 20-minute monthly review where you look at the same few numbers in the same order and make one decision. Systems reduce arguments because they create shared defaults. You’re no longer fighting preferences every week; you’re adjusting a plan you built together. This book rests on that idea: a clear order of operations that turns your financial life into a family wealth operating system.

The first step in building that system is not opening a new account or buying a product. It is seeing reality clearly.

Your Family Wealth Dashboard: The One-Page Reality Check

Think of your family wealth dashboard as the front page of your household's financial newspaper. If you had only one page to understand your money each month, what would need to be on it? Not every line item, just the minimum effective information that lets you make sound decisions quickly. At the end of this chapter scan the QR code for a free Family Wealth Dashboard template.

What Goes on the Dashboard (and What Doesn't)

The dashboard supports decisions, not perfect accounting. It can fit on one page paper, spreadsheet, or app and make your position obvious at a glance. Typically, it includes six categories:

1. Cash: balances in checking and savings available for bills and reserves.
2. Debts: mortgages, student loans, auto loans, credit cards, and other obligations, with interest rates.
3. Investments: total balances in retirement accounts, HSAs used for long-term saving, and taxable investment accounts.
4. Insurance: summary coverage amounts for life, disability, home, auto, and other major policies.

5. Monthly burn rate: what it takes each month to run the household at its current essentials level.
6. Key dates: policy renewals, upcoming large expenses, and planned reviews.

What does not belong initially is every spending category, every transaction, or daily market moves. Those are noise at this level. By focusing on structural numbers, you preserve bandwidth for the questions that matter: Do we have enough cash buffer? Are debt and investing moving in the right direction? Are we protected against obvious risks?

Household Roles and Access

A dashboard helps only if someone owns it and if access to accounts is not trapped in one person's head. In many families, one partner becomes the "money person." Specialization is fine; concentration of knowledge is dangerous.

Clarify three roles. First, the dashboard owner: the person who updates the dashboard before your monthly review. Second, the bill-payer backup: the partner who could, on short notice, pay all critical bills. Third, the document custodian: the person who maintains a list of accounts, policies, and key documents (physically or digitally) and ensures both partners know how to access it.

Underneath these roles is a standard: no mystery accounts. Both partners should have access via a shared password manager or documented process to the financial infrastructure. This is not surveillance; it is resilience. If something happens to one of you, the other should not have to become a detective.

The Monthly "Wealth Review" in 20 Minutes

Once you have a dashboard, you need a rhythm. The goal is a short, predictable check-in that keeps your system current and communication open.

Use a five-step agenda:

1. Review balances across cash, debts, and investments just to get oriented.
2. Check your cash buffer relative to your monthly burn rate.
3. Scan upcoming expenses and key dates and note anything that will affect cash flow.
4. Look at progress on one or two medium- to long-term goals using dashboard totals.
5. Choose one decision for the month—renegotiating a bill, adjusting a contribution, updating a beneficiary and assign a next action with a date.

Put this on the calendar—a recurring Sunday evening, or the first business day after payday and treat it as any important appointment. Twenty minutes once a month prevents the build-up that leads to stressful catch-up marathons.

The First Win: Identify One Leak and One Risk

Early wins build momentum. In your first or second wealth review, look for one leak and one risk.

A leak is a recurring expense that no longer matches your values or usage: a forgotten subscription, a service you can renegotiate, a convenience you no longer need. The goal is alignment, not austerity. Freeing even $50–$100 per month and deliberately redirecting it to your emergency fund, debt payoff, or a 529 turns an invisible drip into visible progress.

A risk is a gap in protection. Look at insurance and beneficiaries and ask: what here would clearly fail us if something went wrong? Coverage that wouldn't cover the mortgage and childcare, a beneficiary who is still a parent instead of a spouse, or no meaningful disability coverage are common examples. You don't have to solve every gap at once. Choose one concrete next step requesting benefit details, updating a form, scheduling a call and put it on the calendar.

With visibility and small wins underway, you are ready for the next layer of your operating system: how money moves through your household week to week.

The Family Cash-Flow Framework That Doesn't Require Perfection

Traditional budgeting often fails not because it is wrong in theory, but because it demands tracking and discipline that collapse under real life. The alternative is not "no structure." It is a framework that guides spending and saving automatically while leaving room for the messiness of kids, careers, and surprises.

Fixed Costs, Flex Costs, and Future Costs

Reframe your spending into three buckets:

- Fixed costs: relatively stable commitments—mortgage or rent, childcare, insurance premiums, minimum loan payments, basic utilities.
- Flex costs: day-to-day choices—groceries, dining out, entertainment, clothes, small home items, kids' activities.
- Future costs: money allocated to tomorrow—emergency fund contributions, retirement and HSA savings, extra debt payments, college savings, major upcoming purchases.

Many families stumble because future costs are treated as optional, funded with "whatever is left." In practice, very little is left. Instead, you decide what proportion of take-home income goes to each bucket, guided by values and goals. If stability and early retirement are priorities, future costs might claim a larger share. In seasons of high childcare, debt or medical expenses, fixed costs will dominate for a while. The targets reflect reality without shame.

The Two-Account Spending Setup

To translate these buckets into behavior without constant tracking, use a two-account setup. One account will be the bills account which will receive all income and pays all fixed and future costs: mortgage, utilities, insurance, minimum loan payments, automatic contributions to savings and investing, and other "must pay" items. The second account—the spending account is for flex costs. Once or twice a month, you transfer a set amount from bills to spending based on your flex target.

The money in the spending account, can use be used for groceries, outings, or small purchases without guilt; obligations and goals are already funded. If the account is low, you get an early warning without jeopardizing the mortgage or retirement contributions. For variable-income households, the same structure applies, but you add a buffer in the bills account and base transfers on a conservative average income, smoothing highs and lows instead of riding them month by month.

A Couple's Script for Setting Spending Boundaries

Systems work best when built on explicit agreement. Before you finalize buckets and transfers, have a values-first conversation, such as: "I want us to feel secure and not panic if something happens at work, and also enjoy life with the kids while they're young. Can we agree that our first priority is keeping the house and covering essentials, second is building three months of expenses, third is staying on track for retirement? Once those are covered, we'll decide together how much fun money we want."

Define personal spending allowances, providing modest amounts each of you can spend monthly with no reporting requirement. This reduces resentment about small purchases and acknowledges that both partners are adults. Agree on how to handle irregular or larger expenses like trips, home projects, and kids' camps, by setting a dollar threshold requiring discussion or deciding such items during the monthly wealth review, which gives you time to think instead of reacting. In the beginning of my wife and I's marriage our threshold was any purchase over $100 would be discussed.

Automation as the Default Setting

Finally, make the system carry as much weight as possible. The most important transfers in your life should be automatic: contributions to your emergency fund until it reaches its target, retirement and HSA contributions, extra payments on high-interest debt, and regular flows between bills and spending accounts.

When new income appears, raises, bonuses, or the end of a major expense like daycare, use a raise-capture rule: automatically increase future-cost allocations before lifestyle expands. Decide in advance that a set share of any permanent income increase goes to saving and investing, and the remainder to lifestyle upgrades.

Automation is not “set it and forget it forever.” Life changes with new jobs, moves, babies, and health issues. All of which are points to revisit your rules. But if your default is that the system runs without constant supervision, you free attention for genuinely complex choices and for the life you are building together. Your cash-flow framework does not have to be perfect; it has to be consistent enough that you can trust it.

With a dashboard that shows reality and a cash-flow system that funds what matters, you have laid the first rails of your family wealth operating system. The next step is building the cushion that keeps this system from derailing when real emergencies—not just unexpected expenses hit. An emergency fund designed for the risks modern families actually face is what you need.

Scan this QR code for your free Family Wealth Dashboard.

Scan Me

Chapter 2: Emergency Funds That Actually Work for Families

If you've ever had a week where everything seemed to hit at once: the car made a new noise, your child spiked a fever, and your company hinted at restructuring—you already understand the difference between "an unexpected expense" and a true disruption. An unexpected expense is a bill you didn't see coming. A disruption is a shift in your family's reality: a job loss, a health event, a major home problem, or a caregiving crisis that rearranges your time, your income, and your stress level all at once. This chapter is about building an emergency fund designed for those disruptions. The fund will cover the occasional flat tire, so that when life veers off script, your family doesn't have to panic, fight, or fall into a debt spiral just to get through the month.

Most families know, in theory, that they "should have an emergency fund." Few have one that matches the risks they face. The problem is rarely laziness; it is vagueness. "We should save more" is not a plan. "We need six months of expenses" sounds precise, but if you don't know what those expenses are or what kinds of emergencies you're planning for you will either underfund the account or give up. Our goal here is to replace that vagueness with a clear, tiered structure, a number you can calculate, and a funding plan that fits your already-busy life. We will also connect your emergency fund to your debt decisions, so you're not putting out fires with one hand and pouring gasoline with the other.

Define Your Family's Real Emergencies

Before you decide how much to save or where to keep it, you need to know what the money is for. "Anything unexpected" is far too broad. If you treat every minor surprise as an emergency, you will drain your fund on convenience rather than stability. A more useful frame is to separate emergencies into three tiers.

Tier 1 is short, sharp shocks: the car repair, the deductible on a medical bill, a broken appliance, or a child's urgent dental work. These are frustrating but don't fundamentally change your life. Tier 2 is income interruption: one or both earners lose a job or have hours significantly cut, or a business owner sees revenues drop sharply. Tier 3 is crisis relocation or caregiving: a parent needs you heavily involved in care, a disaster displaces you from your home, or a serious health event in your household forces major changes in work and childcare.

Families often confuse these tiers and raid the wrong pot of money. A Tier 1 car repair gets covered by the same cash that was quietly supposed to protect you against a layoff. A Tier 2 interruption arrives, and because there was never a separate plan for Tier 1, the "emergency fund" has already been eaten down by a year's worth of irregular bills.

Treating everything as the same level of emergency is like using your retirement accounts to buy groceries: it feels necessary in the moment, but the long-term cost is severe.

Instead, map tiers to tools. Tier 1 is funded by a relatively small and easily replenished buffer. I want you to think roughly one month of essential expenses in a liquid savings account. Tier 2 and Tier 3 rely on larger reserves, insurance, and, in some cases, invested assets with more growth potential. This structure creates a mental boundary: you don't liquidate Tier 2–3 reserves for a Tier 1 problem.

To size those tiers correctly, you need a number: your household burn rate. Burn rate is not what you currently spend; it is what you must spend to keep the family stable. Think of it as your "keep-the-lights-on" cost for one month. It includes housing (mortgage or rent, property taxes if separate), utilities, basic groceries, mandatory insurance premiums, transportation needed for work and school, and minimum payments on debts. It does not include vacations, subscriptions you could pause, or discretionary shopping. If you and your partner disagree about what is "essential," treat that as a useful conversation: in a disruption, which parts of your lifestyle would you actually defend, and which could shrink temporarily?

Once you have that burn-rate number, protection planning becomes concrete. A Tier 1 buffer of one month of essentials is a specific dollar amount, not a guess. A Tier 2 goal of, say, four to six months of burn rate is equally specific. You can now ask: "If one of us lost our job, how many months would this fund cover without panic?" That is far more actionable than "Are we saving enough?" It also clarifies other decisions —how much disability insurance you might need, how comfortable you are with variable income, how aggressively you can invest longer-term money, because you're no longer operating in abstractions.

There is also an emotional job this cash needs to perform. Cash is not only for paying bills; it is for reducing panic. Under acute stress, your brain's ability to weigh long-term trade-offs shrinks. That is when people sell investments in a downturn, tap retirement accounts with penalties, or lean hard on high-interest credit cards. A well-sized emergency fund acts as "family stability insurance." It creates a buffer between a bad event and a bad decision. It also frees you to make intentional moves: taking a lower-paying but healthier job, starting a business carefully, or stepping back from work for a season of parenting or caregiving. Emergency cash supports not just survival, but choice.

Several common traps sabotage this readiness. One is leaving too much in checking with no rules. A large balance mentally labeled "extra" dissolves into lifestyle creep: more dinners out, impulse upgrades, "because it's there." Another trap is the opposite: keeping almost nothing in savings out of optimism or discomfort with idle cash, combined with a quiet belief that "we'll figure it out" if something happens. A third trap is treating credit cards as the emergency plan. Revolving a balance at 18–25% interest is not a plan; it is a very expensive loan that compounds stress. Finally, some families over-invest their emergency funds, chasing higher yields in assets that can fluctuate. When a Tier 1 or Tier 2 event hits during a market downturn, they are forced to sell at losses to pay basic bills. The goal for this money is not maximum return; it is maximum reliability. Looking for a simple high-yield savings account provider will do.

Once you have defined your tiers, calculated your burn rate, and acknowledged the emotional job of cash, you are ready to build. The next step is execution: designing a funding plan that fits your reality.

Build the Fund Without Feeling Like Life Stops

The idea of "three to six months of expenses" can paralyze. If your burn rate is $6,000, that range is $18,000–$36,000. These numbers can feel impossible in your busiest, most expensive years. The way out of paralysis is to think in stages, not perfection.

Stage one is a starter buffer: a small, fast win that separates you from the cliff edge. For many households, an initial target of one month of essential expenses or a fixed figure such as $3,000–$5,000 is enough to change day-to-day stress. This is the money that keeps a surprise dental bill or car repair from turning into a credit card balance that lingers for a year.

To reach that first stage, you do not need to redesign your life. Look for immediate sources. Can you cut or pause one recurring expense like streaming services, a gym you barely use, miscellaneous subscriptions and redirect that money automatically? Is there a tax refund, bonus, or commission check coming that you could commit, in advance, to saving rather than spending? Could you sell unused items in your home and treat the proceeds as a one-time kickstart? How many unused electronics do you have laying around your home that can be sold on Facebook Marketplace or turned in to your cell phone service provider for a credit towards your next bill? Even small, regular steps compound over time; the key is to begin. Think of the starter buffer as installing airbags: it does not make a crash pleasant, but it drastically improves the outcome.

After that initial buffer, progress is mostly about cadence and automation. Relying on willpower saying "we'll save whatever is left at the end of the month" almost always fails. Instead, set a recurring transfer from checking to your emergency savings account that aligns with your pay schedule. If you are paid twice a month, perhaps $150 moves out each paycheck. If you are on weekly payroll, a smaller amount each week. Treat it like a bill, not a leftover. As childcare costs drop, debts are paid off, or raises arrive, increase the transfer. Your family wealth dashboard from Chapter 1 becomes the scoreboard; you can watch the emergency fund line grow, reinforcing that your system is working.

Where you keep this money matters. Emergency funds must obey three rules: safety, liquidity, and separation. The core reserve, especially Tier 1 and most of Tier 2 belongs in a high-yield savings account or equivalent cash vehicle, not a checking account you spend from daily and not in long-term investments that can swing. Checking can hold a small "shock absorber" for truly minor surprises so you are not transferring money back and forth constantly, but the bulk should sit where it is out of sight and out of mind, while still accessible within a day or two. You could name the account something explicit like "Family Emergency Fund" and establish simple withdrawal rules as a couple: what qualifies, who can move money, and how you will replenish it afterward.

You will not always be able to prioritize cash equally. There will be seasons when your emergency fund deserves top billing, and others when maintaining investing habits or capturing a retirement match takes precedence. An unstable job situation, an upcoming move, or a pregnancy often calls for accelerated cash-building. In those windows, it can be rational to slow extra debt payments or discretionary investing in favor of strengthening your reserves. Conversely, when both incomes are stable, your starter buffer is in place, and you are leaving employer retirement match on the table, it can make sense to split new savings between emergency cash and long-term investing. The antidote to endless arguments is a written priority order: for example, "1) Starter emergency buffer; 2) Employer retirement match; 3) High-interest debt; 4) Fully fund Tier 2 reserve; 5) Increase retirement contributions." Agree on that order during calm times and refer back to it during money meetings.

Emergency funds shield you from short-term shocks. But how quickly you can move from survival to progress, especially after a disruption depends on your debt structure. If your fixed obligations are heavy and expensive, even a well-built cash reserve disappears faster. Debt strategy is not just about interest rates; it is about household risk management.

Debt Strategy as Household Risk Management

It is tempting to label debt as "good" or "bad," but a more practical lens is resilience: does this debt make your family more fragile or more flexible? High-interest consumer debt, credit cards, payday loans, store financing at double-digit rates is a financial fire. It demands cash flow every month and grows aggressively if you only make minimum payments. Left unaddressed, it undermines every other part of your plan, including your emergency fund. A fixed-rate mortgage at a reasonable percentage, attached to a housing cost you can comfortably afford, may be stabilizing: predictable, long-term, and tied to a basic need. Student loans sit somewhere in between, depending on rate, remaining term, and how essential the underlying education is to your earning power. Truly risky debt includes variable-rate loans that can jump if interest rates rise, balloon payments that demand a lump sum, or products with opaque fees and penalties. These can turn an otherwise manageable balance sheet into a fragile one.

Once you have categorized your debts in terms of risk, the next question is how to pay them down. Two classic approaches dominate: the avalanche and the snowball. The avalanche method attacks the highest interest rate first while making minimum payments on the rest, then rolls freed-up payments down the list as each debt disappears. Mathematically, this is the most efficient. The snowball method targets the smallest balance first, regardless of rate, creating quick wins. Each payoff delivers a sense of progress that can be powerful if money has felt like a losing battle. A hybrid variant closes out one small balance quickly to build momentum and simplify your list, then switches to avalanche to minimize cost.

For couples, the right choice is not strictly a math problem; it is a behavior and alignment problem. If one partner is highly motivated by rapid visible progress, a pure avalanche strategy may look rational but feel like drudgery. If the other partner cares deeply about efficiency, a pure snowball may feel wasteful. Talk openly about which psychological benefits you value: speed of wins, total savings, or simplification. Then write down the chosen strategy and treat it as the default for at least a year. Constantly switching methods in response to emotions or headlines is more harmful than sticking with a slightly less "optimal" approach consistently.

Refinancing and consolidation offers deserve particular scrutiny. Lowering a monthly payment is not automatically a win if it increases the total cost or ties critical assets to previously unsecured debt. When you evaluate an offer, look at four elements together: the interest rate, total fees, the term length, and what collateral if any is at risk. Extending a loan from five years to ten might cut your payment in half but dramatically increase the total you pay. Turning credit card balances into a home equity loan shifts the risk from your credit score to your house. In some cases, consolidation with a clear, shorter term and lower rate is exactly the right move; in others, it simply rearranges the chairs on the deck. A useful checklist is: "Is the rate meaningfully lower? Are fees reasonable? Is the new payoff date acceptable? What happens if our income drops? Are we comfortable with the collateral at risk?"

Whatever strategy you choose, debt payoff must become a system, not a series of sporadic efforts. Align extra payments with your paydays and automate them so you are not relying on willpower at month-end. Track "debt-free milestones" on your dashboard, balances under a threshold, one card eliminated, a student loan paid off, and acknowledge them during your family finance meetings. Most importantly, pre-decide what happens to each freed-up payment. If a $300 car loan ends and that money simply melts into new lifestyle spending, you have lost a powerful lever. Instead, commit in advance: "When this loan is gone, $200 goes to the emergency fund until we reach Tier 2, and $100 goes to retirement." That way, every debt you eliminate accelerates your move from fragility to freedom.

With a right-sized emergency fund and a deliberate debt strategy, your household becomes much more resilient. You can absorb shocks without panic and convert progress into momentum rather than backsliding. That financial stability also changes the emotional tone of your money conversations. Instead of arguing from a place of constant scarcity and fear, you and your partner can lead from shared plans and clear systems. In the next chapter, we will build on that foundation by focusing on communication: how to turn money talks from tension into trust so that your family wealth operating system is truly a team effort.

Chapter 3: Money Conversations That Build Trust (Not Tension)

Money fights rarely start with a spreadsheet.

They start with a look across the kitchen table when one of you realizes the credit card balance is higher than you expected, when a bonus hits the account and disappears into "miscellaneous," or when a partner says, "I don't even want to talk about it," and walks out of the room. On the surface, you might argue about a purchase, a vacation, or a budget line. Underneath, the real conversation is about safety, respect, autonomy, and control.

If you've ever thought, "We're both smart people. Why does this feel so hard?" you're not alone. Research on couples and money repeatedly finds that conflict isn't driven primarily by arithmetic; it's driven by emotional meaning. One partner hears, "We need to cut back," and feels judged. The other sees a big purchase and feels unprotected. Once you recognize that you're not actually fighting about $200 at Target, but about whether you're on the same team, money talks start to make more sense and they become easier to change.

This chapter gives you something most couples never receive: a clear structure for talking about money as partners instead of opponents. You'll learn how to recognize hidden money stories, run a 30 minute finance meeting that doesn't end in a blow up, and bring a reluctant partner into the conversation without nagging. You don't need to become therapists or financial planners. You need a rhythm, simple scripts, clear roles, and basic rules that turns money from a source of tension into a place where trust grows.

The Hidden Stories Behind Money Disagreements

Every couple brings two invisible ledgers into the relationship. One tracks dollars; the other tracks meaning. You may never have said out loud, "Money means security to me," or "Money is how I buy freedom," but you live those beliefs every day. When those definitions clash and go unspoken, you end up having the same argument in different disguises for years.

For many people, money represents safety. A padded savings account, retirement contributions, and expense tracking feel like protection. For others, money represents freedom and possibility. Travel, generous gifts, and a few "unnecessary" comforts feel like proof that the work is worth it. Put those two in a kitchen together and you can see the collision. The saver thinks, "If we don't buckle down, we're at risk," while the spender thinks, "If we're always counting, we're missing our life."

Childhood experiences, scarcity, sudden job loss, or a family that never talked about bills and always "managed somehow" shape these reflexes. A useful exercise is for each of you to finish three sentences privately and then share: "Growing up, money was...," "Today, money mostly feels like...," and "When I think about our future, money means...." The goal isn't to agree; it's to see what you're actually reacting to.

Most recurring money fights trace back to a small set of triggers. The first is surprise: an unplanned purchase, an overdraft, a "by the way" mention of a big decision that's already been made. The second is ambiguity: no shared rules about what counts as "too much," which account a purchase should come from, or how much is "okay" to spend on kids' activities or eating out. The third is fear: a sense that you're behind, that you wouldn't be okay if a job went away, or that you'll never catch up on debt or retirement. When these combine, tone escalates quickly. One partner becomes the prosecutor; the other becomes the defendant.

Each trigger has a structural fix. Clear budgets and dollar thresholds reduce surprises. A shared dashboard reduces ambiguity. A regular meeting rhythm reduces free floating fear because you're facing reality together instead of alone.

Underneath those triggers sits a deeper tension: what's "fair." In many modern households, income is unequal. One person may stay home with young kids, work part time, or earn less while carrying a heavier mental load: tracking school emails, doctor appointments, family logistics. If you only measure fairness in terms of paychecks, you guarantee resentment. It's more accurate and kinder to acknowledge that your family economy is powered by two kinds of contribution: financial and operational.

A simple script can help: "Even though our incomes are different, I see your work with the kids and the house as what makes my work possible. When we make money decisions, I want us both to have a voice that reflects that." Then, define together what fairness looks like in practice. Will decisions be 50/50 regardless of income? Will you each have personal spending money that's not scrutinized? Clarity here lowers the temperature everywhere else.

Transparency is one of the clearest ways to say, "I'm on your side." That doesn't mean your partner has to love every line item, but it does mean there are no mystery accounts, secret credit cards, or hidden debts "to avoid worrying them." Secrecy may feel protective in the moment; it's corrosive over time. Openness, shared logins stored in a password manager, a simple list of accounts, and mutual visibility into major transactions is a form of care.

If one of you were hospitalized tomorrow, could the other keep the lights on, access insurance, and understand what's where? When you frame transparency as protection for the family rather than surveillance ("I want to make sure either of us could run things if the other is down for a while"), questions become less accusatory and more collaborative.

Once you see the emotional landscape under your disagreements, you're ready for structure. You don't need to "work on money" every night. You need a contained, predictable place to have these conversations so they stop hijacking your entire week.

The 30 Minute Family Finance Meeting

Couples often talk about money in exactly the wrong moments: when they're exhausted, when a bill just arrived, or when they're already angry. Changing when and where you talk is as important as what you talk about. A short, regular meeting on your terms turns money from an ambush topic into a standing appointment you can both prepare for.

Choose a cadence that matches your season of life. For most households, a 30 minute meeting once a month is sufficient. During transitions like a new baby, a job change, a move, an inheritance, or a health issue you may want 20–30 minutes every two weeks. Once or twice a year, do a deeper review that looks at the big picture: insurance, estate documents, and retirement progress. Whatever rhythm you choose, make it specific: "First Sunday of the month at 4 p.m." Put it on the calendar like a medical appointment.

The agenda should be simple enough to remember without notes. One effective structure has five parts:

1. **Dashboard check.** Look at accounts, debts, and cash buffer. You're not judging, just orienting.
2. **Upcoming expenses.** Note travel, kids' activities, renewals, or annual bills that need cash set aside.
3. **Goals progress.** Check your emergency fund, debt payoff, retirement contributions, or college savings.
4. **One decision.** Pick a single priority that needs agreement—a change in automation, a purchase, a payoff plan—and resolve only that.

5. **Next actions.** Decide who will do what, and by when.

If an issue requires more research—refinancing options, a new insurance policy—add it to a "parking lot" instead of arguing in circles. End by thanking each other for showing up and confirming the next meeting. That clear end point matters; it keeps the topic from bleeding into the rest of the evening.

Decision rules keep you from having the same debate over and over. Agree on a dollar threshold above which either partner must check in before spending. For some, that might be $100; for others, $500 or more. The exact number matters less than the shared expectation.

Clarify default priorities in advance, in writing: "Until we have three months of essential expenses in cash, extra money goes first to the emergency fund. After that, we fully capture any retirement match, then tackle high interest debt, then consider college savings or extra mortgage payments." With these defaults, when a bonus appears, you're not negotiating from scratch, you're referring back to your agreed operating system. For major changes like quitting a job, withdrawing retirement funds, or taking on new debt, use a 24 hour pause rule: "If either of us feels uneasy, we'll sleep on it and revisit tomorrow."

Treat documentation as a gift to your future selves. Keep a shared "Family Money Notes" file you both can access. For each meeting, jot down the date, key decisions, the reasons behind them, and next steps. Over time, this modest log becomes a record of your progress and a reference when memories blur: "We decided to prioritize the emergency fund last March because of job instability; now that work is more secure, we can revisit that." Use the notes to track where accounts are held and keep a short list of professional contacts like your financial planner, insurance agent, and attorney so you're not scrambling in a crisis. When you update beneficiaries or estate documents, add a line: what changed and where the new documents live.

After a few of these meetings, you'll likely notice something subtle: even if the numbers aren't perfect, the act of facing them together lowers anxiety. That shared leadership is exactly what you'll need as you move into protection decisions in later chapters.

Before we go there, there's a common complication that deserves its own attention: what if one of you is all in on this, and the other would rather do almost anything else?

When One Partner Isn't Engaged (Yet)

In many couples, one person naturally gravitates toward money management while the other prefers to stay out of the details. That division can work on the surface for a while. But when only one partner understands the system, the family carries a risk: if the "money person" is unavailable, sick, or overwhelmed, no one else can steer. There's also a relational risk, as resentment builds on both sides: "I carry all the burden" versus "You treat me like a child." The solution isn't to force equal enthusiasm; it's to invite meaningful participation on terms that respect each person's temperament.

Start, not with spreadsheets, but with what your partner already cares about. They may light up when they talk about a sabbatical, starting a business, traveling with the kids, or simply not worrying about bills at night. Connect money systems directly to those values. You might say, "I know you don't love the numbers. But that trip you want in three years, or being able to switch careers without panic—this is how we make those possible." Then ask curiosity questions instead of issuing orders: "When you think about our money, what stresses you most?" "What would 'peaceful' look like to you?" Focus on aligning around one shared goal before diving into tactics: "Could we agree that, this year, getting one month of expenses in savings is our joint win?"

Lower the activation energy. Don't invite them to a "financial summit" that sounds like punishment. Invite them to a single, time bounded session: "Would you be willing to sit with me for 20 minutes on Sunday to look at a one page summary of where we are? No decisions, just understanding." Bring visuals instead of cluttered spreadsheets. A clean dashboard that shows cash, debts, and key goals at a glance. Offer two concrete options instead of open ended questions: "Would you rather we meet monthly or every other month?" "After breakfast on Saturdays or one evening after the kids are down?" When people know what to expect and see an end point, they're more likely to show up.

At the same time, define a minimum standard of involvement. At a baseline, both of you should know where the accounts are, how the bills are paid, and who to call if something goes wrong. Both should attend at least quarterly "big picture" meetings where major decisions are reviewed. Both should explicitly sign off on critical protections: life and disability coverage, health insurance choices, and estate documents. Frame this minimum as a safety requirement, not as a referendum on competence: "I'm not asking you to become the money person. I'm asking us to make sure either one of us could run things if we had to."

Sometimes reluctance isn't laziness; it's shame. Maybe there was a past bankruptcy, hidden debt, or a high risk investment that went badly. Dragging old mistakes into the light without care can deepen that shame and entrench avoidance. A more constructive approach is a no blame review: "Let's look at what happened with that credit card last year. What were we trying to do? What did it cost us? What system could we put in place so we don't repeat it?" The focus shifts from character to structure. In situations where conflict feels stuck, if discussions always explode, or one partner simply shuts down consider involving a neutral third party, such as a financial planner used to working with couples or a couples therapist with experience in financial stress.

Once you and your partner can sit together, name your shared "why," and follow a simple meeting structure, you've already done some of the hardest relational work in this book. You've shifted money from an unspoken source of tension to a subject you can handle as a team. In the next part, you'll apply that teamwork to protecting your family's greatest financial asset: the income that powers everything else.

Chapter 4: Protect the Income: Life and Disability Done Right

The easiest way to see why this chapter matters is to imagine a seemingly solid family with two incomes, mortgage on autopay, kids in daycare or sports, retirement contributions humming along, all brought to a halt by one event: a diagnosis, an accident, or a sudden death. The bills do not pause. The kids' needs do not pause. The question that immediately appears is brutally simple: "How does money keep flowing into this household if one of us can't work, or isn't here?" For most families, the car, the home, and even the investment accounts are not the true engine of their plan. The engine is income: the paychecks that quietly fund every piece of the life they've built. This chapter is about defending that engine with clear, rational decisions on life and disability insurance, so you're not gambling your family's future on optimism or employer default settings.

You don't have to love insurance to do this well. You do need a framework that pulls it out of the realm of vague fear and sales language and into the same territory as the rest of your operating system: numbers, timelines, and trade-offs you can understand. We'll treat insurance as income protection, not as a product you "buy once and forget," then examine the main tools—term and permanent life insurance, including indexed universal life (IUL), and disability coverage—with enough clarity that you can make deliberate decisions, document them, and revisit them as your life changes.

Your Family's Income Is the Engine

When people talk about wealth, they often point to visible assets: a house with equity, balances in retirement accounts, maybe a college fund. But for most households in their 30s, 40s, and 50s, the asset that dwarfs all of these is something you can't log into: your human capital. Human capital is the value of all the earnings you're likely to bring in over the rest of your working life. If you are 40 years old, earn $120,000 a year, and plan to work 25 more years, your human capital—before raises—is in the millions. That stream of future paychecks pays the mortgage, keeps childcare in place, funds college, and eventually creates financial capital in your investments. Insurance decisions make sense only when you see them as protecting that stream, not as abstract policies on a shelf. Underinsuring is rarely the result of a conscious decision to take extreme risk; it's more often the default outcome of never sitting down to quantify how much of that income the family truly relies on.

A better frame is to treat life insurance as part of a "needs approach" calculation rather than a guess or a round number someone mentioned at work. The needs approach asks: if you were gone tomorrow, what obligations would your income have been covering, and for how long? That means adding up debts you would want cleared—mortgage, car loans, private student loans, credit cards—plus an income replacement period for your spouse or partner, education goals for children, and final expenses. It's prudent to overestimate rather than underestimate, especially on big monthly items. This approach also recognizes that the need for income replacement usually declines over time as children move out or become self-sufficient or if a surviving spouse later remarries. In contrast, the "human life value" approach estimates the present value of your entire future earnings stream, but for most families, the needs approach is easier to connect to real decisions.

Once you've listed obligations, you subtract anything already there to cushion the blow: existing savings, current life insurance, and any survivor benefits from pensions or Social Security. You also clarify what lifestyle must be preserved versus what is flexible. Does the survivor need to stay in the current home until the youngest graduates, or would moving be acceptable? Do you want to fully fund four years of college for each child, or provide a base that the child supplements with work and aid? A simple stress test—"If I were gone, could my spouse keep the house, keep childcare, and keep retirement on track at least modestly?"—turns an abstract coverage number into a concrete standard.

Insurance, like the rest of the operating system, is not a one-time project. It should change as your family changes. Key life events are natural triggers: marriage, the birth or adoption of a child, buying or upgrading a home, a major change in income, or a health event that alters insurability. A structured way to handle this is to tie an annual insurance review to your family finance meeting: once a year, pull up policies, confirm coverage amounts, and ask, "If something happened this year, is this still enough, too much, or misaligned?" Every time you reach one of those life events, you also review beneficiaries; out-of-date beneficiaries are one of the most common, and most avoidable, wealth-transfer errors.

Thoughtful planning also keeps you out of two extremes. On one side is overbuying: saying yes to every rider and complex permanent policy pitched to you, locking up cash flow in expensive premiums that crowd out emergency savings and investing. On the other side is underbuying or ignoring the topic because it's uncomfortable or because "we have something at work." Employer life coverage is helpful, but it often caps out at one or two times salary, may not be portable if you leave, and can change if the employer changes the benefit. A middle path is to write down a coverage rationale—"We are insuring for X because of Y for Z years"—and keep that note with your dashboard. This turns insurance from an emotional reaction into a deliberate household policy and prepares you to choose specific tools.

Choosing Life Insurance: Term, Permanent, and Clear Decision Criteria

With your needs framed, the next step is understanding the tools themselves. Life insurance, at its core, is a contract: in exchange for a premium, the insurer promises to pay a death benefit to named beneficiaries if the insured dies while the policy is in force. There are several main categories—term life, whole life, universal life, and variable universal life (VUL)—each with different combinations of duration, cost, and savings features. For most families in their highest-need years, term insurance is the workhorse. A term policy provides a pure death benefit for a defined period—10, 20, or 30 years are common. There is no cash value and no investment component, so the premium is generally far lower per dollar of coverage than permanent policies. That makes it well-suited to covering the years when the mortgage is large, kids are dependent, and your human capital is high. Choosing term length becomes an exercise in matching milestones: a 20-year term might carry you until the youngest child finishes college; a 30-year term might carry you to a planned retirement age.

Permanent insurance—whole life, universal life, and VUL—adds a long-duration or lifetime death benefit plus a savings or investment component that can accumulate cash value. Whole life offers fixed premiums, guaranteed death benefits, and a cash value that grows at a rate set by the insurer. Universal life is more flexible on premiums and death benefits, and variable universal life allows the cash component to be invested in market-linked subaccounts. Permanent insurance can be an appropriate tool where the goal is not just to protect against premature death during working years but to guarantee a pool of money whenever death occurs: providing liquidity to pay estate taxes or equalize an inheritance, funding lifelong care for a dependent with special needs, or supporting a specific legacy plan. The trade-offs are higher ongoing premiums, more complex policy mechanics, and the need for long time horizons to make the economics work. A useful rule is to separate your insurance need (income and obligation protection) from your investment goals. If you want market exposure, you have many simpler, more transparent vehicles than the cash-value component of a permanent policy.

Indexed universal life (IUL) is a form of universal life whose cash value growth is linked to a market index, such as the S&P 500, subject to caps, participation rates, and floors. The glossy projections you see—illustrations—are based on assumptions about future index returns and policy costs. Those assumptions can dramatically change actual outcomes. Sensible questions include: What is the current cap on credited interest, and can it be changed by the insurer? What is the participation rate—the percentage of index gains that flow into your policy? What are all the fees and charges, including cost of insurance, policy administration, and riders? How do policy loans work, what rates apply, and what happens if a loaned policy underperforms? How is downside protection actually implemented, and what trade-offs does it imply? Before committing, compare the proposed IUL to a simpler alternative that pursues the same goal—such as term insurance plus investing the difference in low-cost diversified funds—and see which one gives you more control and clarity.

Behind any life insurance decision are paperwork choices that matter as much as the policy itself. Ownership, insured, and beneficiary are three distinct roles. The owner controls the policy—can change beneficiaries, access cash value, and decide whether to keep paying premiums. The insured is the person whose life the policy is based on. The beneficiary receives the death benefit. In some cases, it can make sense for a trust, not an individual, to be the owner or beneficiary, especially where estate taxes, special needs, or blended families are involved. Regardless of structure, outdated beneficiaries are a silent risk. Make beneficiary review a standing item in your annual meeting, especially if your estate plan uses trusts or if you've named guardians for minor children and want life insurance proceeds to support that plan.

Statistically, your family is more likely to face a period where income stops because of illness or injury than because of early death. Your operating system must therefore treat disability coverage as co-equal with life insurance, not an optional extra.

Disability Insurance: The Overlooked Cornerstone

If your human capital is the engine of your plan, disability is the risk that the engine runs at a fraction of previous power—or stops altogether—while your expenses continue. Long-term disability can last months, years, or the rest of a working life. Beyond lost income, there are secondary costs: medical bills not fully covered by health insurance, home modifications to accommodate mobility issues, increased childcare or eldercare, and the logistical strain of caregiving. From a wealth perspective, an extended disability can derail retirement saving, force early withdrawals and penalties from tax-advantaged accounts, and trigger increased debt. Protecting against that risk is therefore a central part of protecting the household's long-term trajectory.

Many employers provide group disability coverage, which is a valuable starting point but often incomplete. The headline replacement percentage—60% of salary, for example—may apply only to base salary, excluding bonuses or commissions. If the employer pays the premium, the benefits may be taxable, meaning your net take-home replacement could be far lower than 60%. The definition of disability matters: an "own-occupation" policy pays if you cannot perform the material duties of your own job; an "any-occupation" policy may only pay if you cannot perform any work for which you are reasonably suited. Benefit duration—how long payments last—is another critical variable; some employer plans cover only a few years, others to a normal retirement age. Group coverage is also typically not portable: change jobs, and your coverage may disappear or reset with different terms.

When you evaluate disability coverage, focus on features that significantly change outcomes. The definition of disability—own-occupation versus any-occupation—is the first. For professionals with specialized skills, own-occupation coverage is usually far more protective. The elimination period—the waiting period before benefits start—should be coordinated with your emergency fund; a longer elimination period typically lowers premiums but requires more cash reserves. Cost-of-living adjustment (COLA) riders can help benefits keep pace with inflation during a long disability. Partial or residual disability provisions may pay a benefit if you can work in a reduced capacity, which often matches real-life scenarios better than an all-or-nothing standard. Each of these elements has a cost, but they define how well the income engine is truly protected.

A simple coverage gap checklist brings this into your dashboard. First, calculate your family's essential monthly costs—the same "burn rate" used for your emergency fund: housing, utilities, food, insurance, minimum debt payments, core transportation, and unavoidable medical expenses. Then, gather your employer disability summary and any individual policies and estimate what monthly, after-tax benefit would be paid if you were disabled. Compare the two numbers. If your essential costs are $7,000 per month and your net projected disability benefit is $4,000, you have a $3,000 monthly gap. In a dual-income household, identify whose income is more critical based on both amount and dependency—who carries the health insurance, who contributes more to long-term goals, and how easily each role could be replaced or reduced. Often, the right sequence is to fully understand

and optimize employer coverage, then explore individual supplemental policies to close the highest-priority gaps.

Document your findings and decisions in your family wealth dashboard. Note which employer policies you rely on, what gaps remain, what steps you will take (requesting plan details, getting quotes for supplemental coverage, building a larger Tier 1 emergency fund to support a longer elimination period), and when you will review again. That way, disability protection becomes part of your operating system, not an uncomfortable flyer you tucked into a desk drawer.

Insurance—life and disability—protects the income that keeps your current life functioning. In the next chapter, you'll extend that protection to the legal and logistical infrastructure that controls what happens if you are gone or incapacitated: wills, powers of attorney, guardianship, and the estate planning basics every parent needs.

Chapter 5: Estate Planning Basics Every Parent Needs

You are loading the dishwasher after dinner when your phone rings. It is a nurse from a nearby hospital. There has been an accident. Your spouse is alive, but unconscious. The nurse needs to know what medications they take and whether they have any advance medical directives on file. A few hours later, another question: who can consent to a procedure? Tomorrow the mortgage is due; next week, the kids' tuition draft hits your checking account. Over the coming days there will be insurance forms, HR paperwork, and decisions about who is allowed to talk to doctors, banks, and schools. In many families, no one knows where anything is, much less who has the authority to act. The result is not just emotional turmoil, it is also practical chaos.

Estate planning is about preventing that chaos. Too often, it is framed as a technical, morbid topic: "what happens when you die." For a household in its peak responsibility years, that framing is inadequate. Proper estate planning is about control and continuity: ensuring that, if something happens to you, the people you love can step in, make decisions, access resources, care for your children, and carry out your wishes without fighting a system you could have organized in advance. In this chapter, we will treat estate planning as a core parenting task and a pillar of your family wealth operating system, not an optional legal accessory you might "get to someday."

The Real Purpose of Estate Planning: Control and Continuity

For parents, the most urgent and most emotionally charged piece of estate planning is guardianship. If you and your co-parent both die or become unavailable, a court must decide who will raise your minor children. If you have not named guardians in a valid document, the judge is left to infer your intentions from whatever relatives show up and argue their case. That can mean uncertainty for your kids and conflict among grandparents, siblings, or former partners. Worse, the "best" choice in the judge's eyes may not be the person whose values, parenting style, and stability you would have chosen.

Naming primary and alternate guardians is how you exercise your parental judgment in advance. It requires a frank discussion: Who shares your values about discipline, education, and faith? Who is realistically able to add your children to their household? Are they willing, not just flattered? Guardianship is not a one-time decision; as your children grow and family circumstances change, your choices may need updating. Failing to choose is, in effect, choosing court involvement by default.

If guardianship is the visible tip of the iceberg, incapacity planning is the mass below the waterline. Many families assume that if one spouse is incapacitated, the other can simply "take over" all decisions. That is not always true. Banks may refuse to let you change accounts or sell property titled solely in your spouse's name. Doctors may limit the information you receive or hesitate to follow your preferences if there is no health care directive or medical power of attorney.

Incapacity documents solve this by granting authority while you are still alive but unable to act. A durable power of attorney gives a trusted person, often your spouse the legal right to manage financial matters: paying bills, dealing with the mortgage company, handling insurance claims. A healthcare proxy or advance directive tells doctors who can make medical decisions for you and what your preferences are for life support, resuscitation, and similar issues. In concrete terms, these documents keep the lights on, the kids in school, and the medical team clear on who is in charge when the family's emotional bandwidth is already stretched thin.

A third, often misunderstood element of control is beneficiary designations. Many key assets like retirement accounts, life insurance policies, sometimes brokerage or bank accounts with transfer-on-death (TOD) instructions pass according to the named beneficiary on file, not what your will says. If your 401(k) still lists a former partner, that person may receive the account even if your will leaves "everything" to your current spouse. If you name minor children directly, a court may need to supervise those assets until they are adults.

Estate planning here is partly about inventory and audit. List every account that allows a beneficiary: workplace retirement plans, IRAs, life insurance, some investment or savings accounts. Then confirm that each designation matches your current intentions and your overall plan. Whenever you experience a major life event: marriage, divorce, birth or adoption of a child, death of a named beneficiary, you should revisit these forms. An "annual beneficiary audit" can be a simple bullet point in your family's year-end review, but it prevents some of the most painful mismatches between intentions and legal reality.

All of this feeds into the broader objective: reducing family conflict through clarity. In the absence of clear, legally effective documents, families fall back on memories and assumptions: "Mom always said..." or "Dad promised me..." Those competing narratives become fuel for resentment and, in some cases, litigation. Estate planning replaces vague intentions with explicit, documented instructions.

It also allows you to choose the right people for formal roles. An executor or personal representative is responsible for carrying out your will, dealing with creditors, and distributing assets. A trustee (if you use a trust) manages assets for others, often over many years. These are jobs, not honors. Competence, reliability, and integrity matter more than birth order or fear of hurt feelings. You can soften the emotional impact by pairing your formal documents with a "values memo" or legacy letter that explains your decisions in plain language. This is not a legal instrument, but it can defuse misunderstandings: "We left more to your sibling because they have special needs" or "We chose your aunt as trustee because of her financial experience, not because we love anyone more or less." Legal clarity plus emotional context is what truly protects relationships.

Once you understand estate planning as a system for control and continuity, the next question is which tools to use. Especially the often-confused pair of wills and trusts.

Wills vs. Trusts: What Most Families Actually Need

For most parents, the starting point is a will. A will is a legal document that communicates your wishes about who receives your assets at death, who will administer your estate, and critically for parents, who will serve as guardian of minor children. It is also the place you name an executor and can outline basic distribution intentions. However, a will does not own your assets during your life, nor does it avoid the legal process called probate.

Probate is the court-supervised procedure for proving that a will is valid, appointing the executor, and overseeing distribution. In many jurisdictions, probate is routine; in others, it can be slow or costly. Either way, it is public: your will and certain details of your estate can become part of the court record. A will does important things for parents such as naming guardians, setting out your distribution plan, and can incorporate basic tax or charitable strategies. It also does have limitations around privacy, timing, and administrative burden.

This is where trusts enter the picture. A living trust (more formally, a revocable living trust) is both a document and a bucket. During your lifetime, you transfer ownership of certain assets like your home, investment accounts, and sometimes bank accounts into the trust. You usually serve as your own trustee, retaining full control: you can buy, sell, spend, and change beneficiaries. The trust document then specifies how those assets should be managed if you become incapacitated and how they should be distributed at your death.

One of the key distinctions between wills and living trusts is that a will only speaks at death and does not house your assets in the meantime, whereas a living trust holds your assets and provides instructions for how they will be managed and distributed. Wills are subject to probate court; a living trust typically allows you to bypass probate for the assets titled in its name, enabling them to be distributed more privately and efficiently. At the same time, a will offers functions a living trust does not: it allows you to name guardians and sometimes express end-of-life wishes, roles a trust cannot fulfill. In practice, many families benefit from using both tools together rather than viewing them as mutually exclusive.

Why might a trust be useful in addition to a will? One major reason is control over timing, especially when your beneficiaries are minors or young adults. You may not want an 18- or 21-year-old to receive a large sum outright. A trust can stagger distributions—perhaps some funds are available for education and health needs, then portions at later ages. Trusts can also provide continuity during incapacity: your successor trustee can step in and manage trust assets if you cannot, without going to court for authority. For families with special situations like blended families, a child with special needs, property in multiple states, or a desire for greater privacy, a trust can reduce friction and protect vulnerable beneficiaries.

However, it is a mistake to think of a trust as a magic switch you flip once. There are costs, complexities, and ongoing responsibilities. Creating the trust is only step one; "funding" it, and retitling assets into the trust's name is essential and often where plans quietly fail. Your home's deed must be updated; brokerage accounts must be opened in the trust's name or retitled; new accounts may need beneficiary language adjusted. This takes time and follow-through.

There is also maintenance: as you open new accounts, refinance a home, or change investments, you have to remember to align these changes with your trust. After major life events like marriage, divorce, a new child, or a move across state lines, your attorney may need to review and amend the documents to keep them effective.

Given these trade-offs, how do you decide what you actually need now? A practical decision checklist starts with triggers. If you have minor children, own a home or other meaningful assets, care about privacy, or have a complex family structure (such as children from prior relationships), you should at least have a will with guardianship provisions, powers of attorney, and health care directives. A trust becomes more compelling when you want to avoid probate for most assets, expect your beneficiaries will need structured distributions, have property in more than one state, or anticipate that incapacity management will be important.

If you are unsure, it is often wise to start with a solid will plus directive package and correct beneficiary designations. You can add a trust later as your assets and complexity grow. The key is to document today's decision—"We will revisit whether to add a trust at our annual review in three years or if we buy a second property"—so the question does not vanish into good intentions.

Once you have the right documents, they must be usable. In a crisis, no one has the bandwidth to dig through random file drawers. This is why your estate planning system needs a physical and digital home.

The Emergency & Estate Binder: Make the Plan Findable

Imagine that nurse calling from the hospital again. This time you walk to a single shelf, open a clearly labeled binder, and pull out your spouse's health care directive, insurance card copies, and a one-page summary of key contacts. That is the function of an emergency and estate binder: it translates your abstract "plan" into a practical, accessible tool for the people who will need it most.

What goes inside? At minimum, you want identification documents (copies of birth certificates, marriage certificate, passports, Social Security cards), core financial and legal records (insurance policies, recent tax returns, property deeds or leases, mortgage documents, account summaries, and your wills and any trusts), and essential medical information (health insurance cards, current medications with dosages, medical histories, and contact information for doctors and pharmacies). You also need an organized list of emergency contacts: close family, key friends, employers or HR contacts, school administrators, and utility providers. A concise "If something happens" instruction page at the very front should tell a spouse, adult child, or trusted friend what to do first: who to call, where the master password file is, how to reach your attorney or financial advisor.

Storage is a balancing act between security and accessibility. A fire-resistant, waterproof home safe is often a good primary location for physical originals and your binder. If you use a safe-deposit box at a bank, be careful: in some jurisdictions, the box can be sealed upon death, making immediate access difficult. Digital backups are equally important. Scanning key documents and storing them in encrypted digital storage and protected by a strong password manager means you can access them in an evacuation or disaster. The binder itself can contain instructions for accessing the password manager, not the passwords themselves, so that a spouse or designated helper can step in without exposing you to unnecessary risk during normal times. Whatever system you choose, write down where the binder and any digital backups live, and test whether your spouse or another trusted person can actually open them without your help.

That leads to the next question: who should know about this system, and how much should they know? At minimum, both partners in a household must have full awareness and access. It is not acceptable for one spouse to be the sole keeper of all knowledge. Beyond that, designating a single backup person like a sibling, close friend, or professional advisor who knows that “if something happens, the documents are in X location and here is how to open them” creates a second line of resilience. Guardians and executors should be told about their roles well in advance, and you can decide how much financial detail to share based on family dynamics and the ages of your children. The goal is to avoid a situation where someone is legally responsible but practically uninformed.

An estate binder is only as good as its last update. The maintenance burden does not have to be heavy if you tie it to events and routines. When you move, change jobs, open a new account, or have another child, add “update the binder and dashboard” to your checklist. At least once a year, ideally during the annual family wealth reset you will design later in this book. Pull out the binder and scan for outdated information: replaced insurance policies, closed accounts, new doctors, changed schools. Your family wealth dashboard can serve as the living index: if an account appears on the dashboard, there should be a reference to it in the binder, either as a statement or a note on how to access it. The combination of an up-to-date dashboard and a well-maintained binder turns your estate planning from a stack of paper into an operating system that others can run if necessary.

With guardians named, documents in place, and an estate binder assembled, you have built a solid protection layer around your family. The next dimension of protection is less obvious but equally important: managing your tax exposure intentionally, so that more of what you earn and invest remains available to fund the future you are building and, eventually, the legacy you plan to leave.

Chapter 6: Tax-Smart Decisions for Busy Households

Taxes are one of the few expenses your family will definitely have every year and, unlike your mortgage or grocery bill, they're often invisible until it's too late to change them. You see the withholdings on your paystub, maybe grumble at your property tax statement, and then in March or April you hand a stack of documents to a preparer or a software program and hope for the best. For many busy families, that's the entire "tax plan." By the time you or your preparer are filling in boxes on a return, almost every meaningful decision has already been made. The dollars were earned in particular ways, routed through certain accounts, and spent or given according to habits, not strategy. Filing simply reports the story that already happened.

This chapter is about rewriting that story on purpose. You do not need to become a tax expert, and you do not need exotic loopholes to materially improve your outcomes. You do need a basic mental model for how taxes work in a household, a short list of levers you can reasonably pull, and a simple rhythm for checking in before the year is over. When you treat taxes as another line item you can influence, like insurance premiums or childcare costs, you stop feeling ambushed and start using the system the way it was actually designed: to reward certain behaviors, especially long term saving and thoughtful giving, and to give you options about when and how different dollars are taxed.

Taxes as a Line Item You Can Influence

Taxes are not a static fact; they're the result of how your income, savings, and spending show up under the tax rules where you live. You cannot control every variable, but you can control enough that the difference over a decade can be large for a typical professional household and far larger for families with higher incomes or business interests. Large institutions understand this and integrate tax decisions across investing, estate planning, charitable giving, and business moves. Your version is simpler but rests on the same foundation: understand the key levers, plan ahead, and coordinate taxes with the rest of your plan.

A useful way to organize those levers is: Earn, Save, Spend. On the "earn" side, your choices include how much tax is withheld from each paycheck, how bonuses are timed and taxed, and how you handle side income. Adjusting your Form W 4 so that withholding is roughly aligned with your actual liability smooths cash flow and avoids both big bills and unnecessarily large refunds. If one of you has irregular income —commissions, consulting, or a small business, you may need quarterly estimated payments; treating those as a fixed percentage of each check, automatically swept to a "tax bucket," keeps surprises low.

On the "save" lever, the accounts you use like a 401(k), IRA, HSA, and others, determine whether dollars are deducted, deferred, or taxed later at potentially lower rates. "Spend" covers deductions and credits, plus the timing of certain expenses. Clustered charitable gifts, for example, can push you above the standard deduction in one year instead of being wasted in several, and some education or energy related credits require action before December 31.

To use these levers intelligently, you need to understand how your income is actually taxed. Many people believe a myth: "If I get a raise and it pushes me into the next bracket, I'll lose money because all my income is taxed at that higher rate." That is not how marginal tax brackets work. Your marginal rate is the rate applied to your last dollar of income in a given bracket; your effective rate is the blended average across all your income. Crossing into a higher bracket means only the dollars above that threshold are taxed at the new rate; all the income in the lower brackets still enjoys their lower rates. Misunderstanding this leads employees to turn down overtime, hesitate about promotions, or make rushed year end spending decisions to "avoid going into a higher bracket" when the extra income would still raise take home pay. Once you see the distinction, you can evaluate decisions like bonus elections or Roth conversions more clearly.

Just as important is separating tax planning from tax filing. Filing is backward looking: you gather forms, report what occurred, and calculate what you owe or are owed. Planning is forward looking: you decide, during the year, how much to contribute to retirement accounts, whether to accelerate or defer certain income or expenses, how to structure side work, and whether to alter withholdings. Your family operating system should include at least one mid year tax check and a simple year end review. Those sessions are not about reading the tax code; they're about holding your dashboard up next to last year's return and asking a few questions: Are we on track for our contribution targets? Has our income changed enough that we should adjust withholdings? Are there credits or deductions we can still qualify for with modest, values aligned changes? Should we be finalizing a charitable gift we already intend to make?

At some point, many families cross a complexity line where "do it yourself with software" stops being the best use of time or risk budget. Triggers for seeking professional help include business or self employment income, rental properties, equity compensation (stock options or restricted stock units), significant realized capital gains, or complex giving and estate strategies. When you reach that line, your goal is not just to outsource box filling; it is to hire a partner who will coordinate tax strategy with your broader plan. Walking into that relationship prepared by bringing your household dashboard, prior year returns, a list of upcoming goals, and specific questions, makes the engagement far more effective. Clarify scope: will this professional simply prepare your return, or will they model the tax impact of different contribution levels, Roth conversions, or business decisions and help you decide among them?

Once you see taxes as connected to everything else, the next natural question is: if you're going to save anyway, which accounts give you the best tax treatment, and in what order should you fund them?

Retirement Accounts, HSAs, and the Order of Operations

Tax law rewards families who build long term savings inside certain accounts. For most employed households, the workhorse is an employer sponsored retirement plan such as a 401(k) or 403(b). If your employer offers a matching contribution, capturing that match is almost always your first tax advantaged priority. A match is, functionally, a guaranteed return: if you contribute 5% of your salary and your employer adds another 5%, you've doubled that portion of your savings before any market growth. Your contributions often reduce current taxable income in a traditional account, and growth is tax deferred. Treat "enough to get the full match" as a baseline default, automated through payroll so you do not have to make a monthly choice.

Beyond the match, you'll usually decide between traditional (pre tax) and Roth (after tax) contributions. The analytical question is not "Which is best?" but "When are we likely to face higher tax rates—now or later?" If you are in your peak earning years, facing relatively high current marginal rates and expecting a lower income in retirement, traditional pre tax contributions may create more value by deferring income into a lower rate future. If you are early in your career, currently in a low bracket, or believe future tax rates will be higher, Roth contributions, which means you'll be paying tax now to enjoy tax free withdrawals later can be attractive. Many households sensibly do some of both, building "tax diversification" so that future retirees can choose from both taxable and tax free buckets depending on the landscape. The key is to make an explicit choice in the context of your life stage and goals, not default blindly.

One of the most powerful tools, especially for families with high deductible health plans, is the Health Savings Account. Properly used, an HSA combines three tax advantages: contributions can be made pre tax, growth is tax deferred, and withdrawals for qualified medical expenses are tax free. To access these benefits, your health insurance must meet specific high deductible criteria and you cannot be enrolled in Medicare. You can use the account for current out of pocket costs, but some families deliberately pay those costs from cash flow, save receipts, and allow the HSA to compound for decades, later reimbursing themselves tax free in retirement. That strategy demands careful recordkeeping and a long term mindset, but the tax arithmetic is compelling.

Because there are multiple attractive options, many couples stall out in analysis paralysis. An "order of operations" simplifies decisions. A reasonable starting waterfall for many households is:

1. Build a basic emergency buffer so that short term shocks do not push you into high interest debt.
2. Contribute enough to capture the full employer match.
3. Aggressively pay down any high interest consumer debt (credit cards, personal loans).
4. Increase core retirement contributions toward your target savings rate.
5. If education funding is a priority, direct additional savings to 529 plans or other vehicles.
6. Add taxable investing for additional flexibility.

Households with unstable income might temporarily prioritize a larger cash cushion before adding more to long term accounts; late starters might push retirement contributions higher and accept a more modest education funding goal. What matters is that you write down your chosen waterfall on your dashboard so that each new dollar has a predetermined "job." Once money is flowing into these accounts according to a clear order, you have solved half the tax puzzle: you are routing dollars through structures that, by design, reduce your lifetime tax burden. The other half is temporal: making sure that, over the course of the calendar year, you have neither left obvious opportunities on the table nor set yourself up for an unwelcome bill next spring.

Year-End Moves That Reduce Regret

The last months of the year are when planning and filing meet. By that point, most major income events are known, but you still have time to adjust contributions, withholdings, and certain types of spending. A brief year end review can convert a vague "we'll see what the refund looks like" approach into a targeted set of moves that align taxes with your operating system.

Start with withholding and estimated taxes. Pull a recent paystub for each working spouse and look at year to date income and tax withheld. Compare that to a rough projection of total income for the year—salaries, bonuses, side work, investment income. If one of you received a sizable bonus, changed jobs mid year, or added freelance income, withholding may overshoot or undershoot the actual liability. A simple adjustment to your W 4 for the remaining pay periods can reduce the risk of penalties for underpayment or of having thousands of dollars sitting with the government interest free until you file. If you pay estimated taxes on self employment or rental income, true up your planned fourth quarter payment with reality rather than guess.

Next, review your progress toward key contribution targets. Are you on track to hit the 401(k) or 403(b) amounts you committed to, or did contribution percentages lag after a raise or parental leave? Are you using an HSA this year and, if so, are contributions pacing toward the annual limit? Are there opportunities to top up an IRA or 529 plan in a way that fits your cash flow framework? In more complex situations such as very high incomes, large capital gains, or concentrated stock positions, professionals sometimes coordinate year end tax loss harvesting or Roth conversions. Your version may be simpler, but the principle is identical: pause in November or December to ask, "If we do nothing else before December 31, what obvious benefits are we leaving on the table?"

Year end is also a natural moment to align generosity with tax reality. Decide on an annual giving target. Whether a dollar amount or a percentage of income as an expression of your family mission. Then choose the most effective vehicles, from simple cash donations to appreciated securities or donor advised funds, depending on your situation and the thresholds at which itemizing becomes worthwhile. For households no longer itemizing, the primary benefit is values alignment, not tax savings; for others, bunching multiple years' worth of gifts into a single tax year, then taking the standard deduction in off years, can increase the tax impact of generosity without changing the underlying level of support. Involving older children in choosing one or two causes and explaining, in simple terms, how gifts translate into impact integrates legacy teaching into a financial routine.

Finally, use the end of the year to organize for the next one. Update your family dashboard with the final balances in major accounts and note any changes in employers, benefits, or insurance. Place electronic or paper copies of W 2s, 1099s, mortgage interest statements, and other likely tax documents in a single digital folder or physical envelope as they arrive. Confirm that your emergency and estate binder reflects any new accounts or policy changes. Schedule your annual family wealth reset, which will be a deeper review in which you'll revisit coverage, contributions, and longer term strategy, so that it happens on purpose, not when you vaguely remember you "should probably look at the finances again."

Tax smart decisions will not, by themselves, build your family's wealth. But they are a powerful multiplier. Every dollar you do not send unnecessarily to the tax authorities is a dollar that can strengthen your emergency reserves, accelerate debt payoff, buy more compounding time in a retirement account, or fund opportunities for your children. By treating taxes as an integrated part of your operating system and understanding the earn/save/spend levers, using advantaged accounts in a disciplined order, and running a brief year end review, you convert a source of anxiety and confusion into another area of confident leadership. With the tax plumbing in place, you're ready to choose and manage investments in a way that supports your goals without inviting unnecessary risk or drama.

Chapter 7: Investing Fundamentals for the Family's Future

Investing can feel like the point where family finance shifts from concrete ("pay this bill, fund that account") to abstract. Numbers become projections, jargon appears, and headlines scream about crashes and bubbles. In this chapter, we are going to strip investing back down to its real job: turning today's surplus into tomorrow's options without putting your family's stability at risk. You don't need to become a market expert or enjoy reading financial news. You do need a handful of concepts, a simple written plan, and the discipline to follow that plan when your emotions would rather do something else.

You've already worked on cash flow, emergency reserves, debt, tax-smart accounts, and basic protection. Investing sits on top of that foundation. It's how college gets funded, how retirement becomes "work optional," and how you create flexibility for your future self. We'll begin by clarifying what investing actually is and what it isn't. Then we'll turn those ideas into a short, practical family Investment

Policy Statement (IPS). Finally, we'll translate the IPS into specific choices: which kinds of funds to use, how to think about "active vs. passive," and when to bring in a professional. By the end, you will be able to look at your investment accounts and say, "I know why we own this, how we expect it to behave, and what we'll do when markets move."

What Investing Is (and Isn't)

At its core, investing is the decision to delay some consumption today so that your future self and your future family can afford more choices later. You give your money a job: to participate in the growth of businesses, the income from bonds, and the broad progress of the economy over time. That job necessarily involves uncertainty. There is no way to earn higher returns over decades without accepting that the value of your investments will fluctuate in the short term. Speculation, by contrast, is about short-term prediction and excitement: trying to guess where a stock, sector, or coin will move next. A family wealth system is built on investing, not speculation. Your job is not to outsmart markets; it is to harness them in a way that matches your goals and your tolerance for temporary discomfort.

Risk is not just the chance of losing money. It is also the chance of not having enough when you need it. Time horizon is the bridge between those two sides of risk. For retirement, your time horizon might be 20 or 30 years. For a toddler's college fund, perhaps 15 years. For a home renovation you want to do in two years, the horizon is short. The longer your time horizon, the more volatility you can afford to tolerate, because you have time to ride out downturns. This is why it is usually appropriate to hold a significant portion of retirement savings in stock-based investments, but wholly inappropriate to invest next year's property tax payment in stocks. A simple rule: if you will need the money within about five years, you should be very cautious about exposing it to market swings; stability matters more than return.

Diversification is how you take that necessary risk and make it survivable. Imagine your family's investments as a convoy traveling through unpredictable weather. Putting everything in a single stock or sector is like loading your entire family onto one small boat; if it hits a storm, everyone is in trouble. Diversification spreads risk across many companies, industries, countries, and asset types such as stocks, bonds, and cash-like instruments. When one area struggles, others may be stable or rising. This doesn't eliminate the possibility of loss. Markets can and do fall together but it reduces the chance that one bad bet wipes out years of effort. For a family with real goals and dependents, diversification is not a "nice to have." It is the seatbelt that allows you to drive at an appropriate speed.

Fees and friction are quieter, but no less important. Every mutual fund and exchange-traded fund (ETF) charges an expense ratio. Advisors may charge a percentage of assets or a flat fee. Frequent trading can incur transaction costs and, in taxable accounts, trigger capital gains taxes. One percent in annual fees sounds small until you compound it for 20 or 30 years. A higher-cost fund or advisory structure must justify itself by clear value: better planning, behavior coaching, tax integration, or access to strategies you genuinely need. When in doubt, prefer simpler, lower-cost options that provide broad diversification. Complexity often masks cost, and friction quietly erodes what compounding is trying to build.

The most underappreciated driver of returns, however, is behavior. Many investors own reasonably diversified portfolios in theory but sabotage themselves in practice by selling in panic after declines, chasing last year's winners, or constantly tinkering in response to headlines. Over time, these behavior gaps can matter more than the choice between two decent funds. That is why this book emphasizes systems: you want your decisions about contribution levels, risk, and asset mix to be made calmly, in advance, and then implemented mechanically. The family meetings and dashboard you've already set up are part of this behavioral infrastructure. The final piece is a brief written policy that tells you what to do when your feelings are loud and the market is noisy.

Your Family Investment Policy Statement (IPS)

Institutional investors, pensions, endowments, and family offices operate with an Investment Policy Statement. It is not a sales brochure or a prediction; it is a rulebook. Your family deserves the same clarity. A good IPS is short enough to read in a few minutes but specific enough to guide real choices. If you and your spouse are not clear on what the money is for, you will inevitably pull in different directions when trade-offs arise.

Begin your IPS by defining the "why" and the goals. List your top long-term objectives: retirement at a roughly specified age range, helping with children's education, maintaining flexibility to change careers or locations, and perhaps leaving a legacy. Next to each goal, assign a rough time horizon ("20–25 years," "10–15 years") and a priority ranking ("critical," "important," "nice-to-have"). Then write a one-paragraph purpose statement in plain language, something like: "Our family uses investing to create long-term security, fund education opportunities for our children, and allow work to be optional in our 60s, while accepting normal market ups and downs in exchange for long-term growth." This paragraph becomes the standard you can return to when fear or greed tries to rewrite your plan in the moment.

The heart of the IPS is your target asset allocation—the mix between growth assets (primarily stocks) and stabilizing assets (bonds and cash equivalents). Think of this as your main risk dial. More stocks mean higher expected long-term returns and larger short-term swings; more bonds and cash mean lower expected returns and smaller swings. Use your time horizons and temperament together: a couple in their 30s or early 40s saving primarily for retirement might choose a stock-heavy allocation, recognizing that their portfolio value will fluctuate; a couple in their late 50s may tilt more toward bonds to reduce the impact of a major downturn just before retirement. The key is not to chase an "optimal" allocation but to choose one you can stick with during a bad year. A theoretically perfect allocation that you abandon in a downturn is worse than an "imperfect" one you can maintain.

Once you have the allocation, you need contribution rules and automation. Decide, in writing, how much of your income will be directed to investments and in what sequence (tied back to the "funding waterfall" you built in the tax chapter). For example, "We will contribute at least 12% of gross household income to retirement accounts, capturing the full employer match first, then Roth or traditional IRAs, then any additional contributions via taxable accounts as cash flow allows. When either partner receives a raise, at least half of the increase in net pay will go to increasing contributions." Then put these rules on autopilot through payroll deductions and automatic transfers. The aim is to remove as many decision points as possible. You don't want each paycheck to trigger a debate; you want the default to be progress.

Your IPS must also address what happens when markets move sharply both down and up. Set a rebalancing schedule, such as once per year, where you look at your actual allocation and compare it to your target. If one asset class has grown far beyond its intended weight, you shift new contributions or, if necessary, sell and buy to bring the mix back in line. This disciplined "sell what's become too large, buy what's become relatively cheap" behavior is the opposite of emotional reacting. Also write a simple "panic plan": for example, "If markets decline 20% or more, we will not sell based on fear. We will re-read this IPS, review our time horizons, and, if cash flow allows, increase contributions to take advantage of lower prices. We will only reconsider our allocation if our time horizon or life circumstances have truly changed." Define in advance the limited circumstances that justify real changes. Possibly retirement within five years, a major health event, or a permanent income shift so that routine volatility does not masquerade as a reason to overhaul the plan.

Treat this IPS as a living document. As life evolves, children grow, careers change, and inheritance arrives you revisit and update it deliberately, not reactively. The question is always: "Given who we are now and what we're trying to accomplish, is this still the right rulebook?" Keeping that conversation explicit prevents the drift that undermines many long-term plans and prepares you for the deeper retirement analysis in the next chapter.

Selecting Investments Without Getting Lost

With the IPS in place, you now need actual investments that implement your allocation. Here, simplicity is your ally. Most families can meet their goals with a small number of diversified, low-cost funds. Broad-market index funds and ETFs hold hundreds or thousands of securities inside a single vehicle. A total U.S. stock market fund gives you exposure to the whole domestic market; an international stock fund adds foreign exposure; a core bond fund holds a diversified basket of government and high-quality corporate bonds. For many households, three to five such funds across their various accounts are enough. This minimalism reduces maintenance, lowers the likelihood of overlap and confusion, and makes it much easier to see whether you are actually following your IPS.

Bonds and cash-like investments play a specific role: they are the stabilizers and liquidity providers. Money you need within a few years for home repairs, tuition, or early retirement withdrawals should lean heavily toward these safer assets. While their long-term returns are lower than stocks, their value tends to fluctuate less, which becomes crucial when you are spending from the portfolio rather than just contributing. Structurally, you might think in layers: long-term growth money in stock-heavy funds, intermediate-term needs in bond funds, and very short-term needs in cash and high-yield savings.

You will encounter the debate between "active" and "passive" investing. Active management means a person or team is making ongoing decisions about which securities to buy and sell, aiming to outperform a benchmark. Passive investing typically means buying funds that track an index and holding them, accepting "the market" return for that slice. Passive strategies usually have lower costs, more transparency, and fewer taxable events, and they remove a lot of emotion by design. Active strategies may offer the potential for outperformance or risk management but introduce manager risk, higher fees, and a need for monitoring. For busy families, the most important choice is consistency with your IPS: choose an approach you understand, that you believe in enough to stick with when performance temporarily lags, and that does not require more time and attention than you realistically have.

Target-date and other "managed" options can be helpful shortcuts for those who want even less complexity. A target-date fund is designed to adjust its stock/bond mix over time, becoming more conservative as the stated target year (usually your expected retirement year) approaches. Inside a single fund, you get diversification and an automated glide path. The trade-offs are that the glide path might not match your personal risk tolerance, fees can vary, and using multiple target-date funds across accounts can inadvertently distort your overall allocation. A reasonable standard is "good enough": if a well-chosen target-date fund in your 401(k) allows you to save consistently and sleep at night, that may be preferable to a custom portfolio you never quite maintain.

If you choose to work with an advisor, vetting them should be as systematic as choosing investments. Ask how they are compensated—fee-only (a transparent fee for advice), fee-based, or commission-based and what potential conflicts of interest exist. Request a written plan that addresses more than just investing: does it integrate tax considerations, insurance, estate planning, and your family's specific goals? During conversations, pay attention to whether they explain recommendations in plain language and respect your values, or whether they default to jargon and product pitches. A strong advisor relationship is less about access to clever investments and more about having a thinking partner who supports your system, helps you avoid behavioral mistakes, and collaborates with you on life-stage adjustments.

The purpose of investing is not to win a game against strangers; it is to fund the real lives of people you care about. The question is not "What did the market do this quarter?" but "Are we following our plan, contributing at our chosen rate, and staying aligned with our goals?" With these fundamentals in place, clear definitions of risk and time horizon, disciplined diversification, cost awareness, a written IPS, and simple building-block investments you are ready to tackle the next big question: whether your retirement trajectory matches the future you are working so hard to create.

Chapter 8: Retirement Planning During the Most Expensive Years

Every month, the retirement line on your paystub quietly marches on, right alongside the grocery bill, daycare draft, mortgage, and sports registration fees. You are contributing "something" to the 401(k). You've told yourself you'll "really focus on retirement" once daycare ends, or once the next promotion hits. And yet a nagging thought remains: What if "later" comes too fast? How do you fund a future you can't see while still paying for a life that's in your face every day?

This chapter is about putting structure around that tension. You are in the most expensive years of your life. You're experiencing peak child costs, often peak housing costs, sometimes helping aging parents, all while knowing you should be building the engine that will fund the next 30–40 years. Rather than asking you to choose between "enjoy life now" and "never spend a dollar," we'll build an analytical framework: define what "enough" actually means for your household, run a simple retirement gap analysis, and then overlay the reality of multi generational responsibilities. The aim is not a perfect forecast; it is a clear, defensible plan you can explain to your spouse in one page and actually execute in the middle of a busy season.

Define "Enough": Your Retirement Number and Timeline

Planning for retirement becomes paralyzing when it's treated as a single magic number or a hard stop at age 65. A more useful lens is freedom of choice. For many families, the true goal is "work optional": having enough assets and income that paid work becomes a choice rather than an obligation. That might look like one partner shifting to part time at 60, both taking lower paid but more meaningful roles, or stopping traditional employment entirely. Phased retirement—reducing hours over several years, consulting, or changing careers—can dramatically reduce the nest egg required, because you're still earning and not drawing as heavily from savings early on. When you frame retirement as a spectrum of flexibility instead of a cliff, you can choose more realistic targets and reduce today's stress: you are not deciding "never work again," you are designing when and how work becomes optional.

To estimate "enough," you do not need a spreadsheet with 74 rows of expense categories in 2053 dollars. You need a clear distinction between spending needs and spending wants. Baseline needs cover essentials: housing, food, utilities, basic transportation, insurance, and modest healthcare and personal spending. Wants are the upgrades: travel, hobbies with real price tags, more charitable giving, helping adult children with big milestones. In practice, needs might be 60–80% of your current total spending, adjusted for kids leaving the payroll and work related costs (commute, childcare) disappearing. Healthcare may rise and you may want more spending on experiences. Thinking in ranges—"we'd be fine on $X, comfortable on $Y, and delighted on $Z"—is more robust than clinging to a single precise future budget that will surely be wrong.

Your time horizon and current savings rate are the two levers that matter most. If you have 25–30 years until you want work to be optional, compounding can do substantial heavy lifting with modest, consistent contributions. If you are 10–15 years out and starting late, the math is unforgiving: higher contribution rates, a willingness to work longer, or a willingness to accept a leaner lifestyle will be required. The gap between your current trajectory and your desired outcome is a quantifiable concept, not a vague worry. If you keep saving 8% of income and your projections show that only supports your "needs only" lifestyle at 72, but you want "comfortable" at 67, there is a defined gap. You can close it by increasing your savings rate, adjusting your target retirement age, or revising lifestyle expectations. The key is to choose one lever to change this quarter, not to oscillate among all three without action.

Social Security is a crucial component of this analysis, but it should be treated as one input, not the entire plan. Benefits are real and can cover a meaningful portion of baseline needs, especially for couples with two work histories. However, timing dramatically affects the amount: claiming early at 62 locks in a permanent reduction; delaying up to age 70 can significantly increase your benefit and reduce the risk of outliving your assets, especially for the higher earner. A conservative stance assumes: (1) benefits will exist, (2) your personal estimate from the Social Security Administration is a guide, not a guarantee, and (3) if your household has longevity, delaying the higher earning spouse's benefit is often attractive. You want a rational narrative such as: "We are planning as if Social Security will cover roughly 25–35% of our essential needs, with the balance coming from our own savings and any part time work."

Once you have this "enough" framework—a target age or range, a needs vs. wants spending band, and a conservative view of Social Security—you are ready to quantify the distance between here and there.

The Retirement Gap Analysis (Simple, Not Fancy)

A retirement gap analysis is the structured comparison between the income you are on track to have in retirement and the income you will likely want. Even a straightforward version you do at the kitchen table will be far superior to guessing. The first step is to gather inputs: list your current retirement account balances (401(k), 403(b), IRAs, Thrift Savings Plan, etc.), any pensions you've earned, and your spouse's equivalents. Add up your current annual contributions, including employer match. Then note your target retirement age (or range) and the "needs" and "comfortable" annual spending levels you defined earlier. This is not a tax return; it is a high signal snapshot.

Next, choose assumptions about growth and inflation. Many DIY calculators mislead people by defaulting to rosy numbers. Instead of a single best case growth rate, pick a range—perhaps a conservative 4–5% real (after inflation) return for a diversified portfolio, recognizing that actual outcomes will vary. Assume a modest long term inflation rate when translating future dollars back into today's terms. The point is not to predict markets; it is to avoid building a plan that only works if everything goes right. Some tools describe methods for calculating retirement income using projected balances and withdrawal rules such as the "4% rule," which suggests a retiree might be able to withdraw about 4% of their portfolio annually without a high risk of depletion. Treat such rules as rough context, not guarantees.

With your inputs and assumptions, you—or a calculator—can project a rough future portfolio value at your target age and translate that asset base into annual income. Compare that figure, plus estimated Social Security and any pension income, to your "needs" and "comfortable" bands, and identify the gap, if any. Suppose your projection shows that, with current saving, you will likely support $55,000 per year of inflation adjusted withdrawals plus Social Security, and your "needs" band is $50,000 with "comfortable" at $70,000. You are on track for "fine but not generous." That is very different from being on track for only $30,000 when your needs are $50,000. The purpose of the gap analysis is to expose mismatches early enough that you can still move the levers.

Rather than trying to change everything, select one main adjustment lever. Increasing your contribution rate by even 1–2 percentage points of income, especially if you're earlier in your career, can materially narrow the gap over time. If your plan offers automatic escalation, enable it so contributions rise by 1% each year until you reach your target. If your analysis shows that even aggressive saving won't fully close the gap by your ideal age, consider extending your timeline by a few years—perhaps working to 68 instead of 65, or planning for a phased retirement period. Alternatively, revising your lifestyle goal from "multiple international trips every year" to "regional travel plus one big trip every few years" may bring "comfortable" down to a level your projected assets can support. The point is to decide intentionally, not by default.

Whatever adjustment you choose, lock it in with systems instead of willpower. If you decide to raise your 401(k) contribution from 8% to 10%, submit the change to HR or through your plan website immediately—don't leave it on a task list. Update your family dashboard to reflect the new contribution rate and projected impact. Schedule a quarterly 20–30 minute check in where you and your spouse briefly review balances, contribution levels, and any life changes that might affect the plan. Document the rationale—"We increased to 10% to close a projected $8,000/year gap by age 67"—in your Investment Policy Statement and money notes. Over time, the gap analysis becomes a living tool: you re run it every few years, adjust one lever, automate, and move on.

The Sandwich Generation Plan: Kids, Parents, and Boundaries

Retirement planning does not occur in a vacuum; it sits in the middle of competing demands from two other generations. Many readers are simultaneously saving for college, paying for braces, or helping adult children launch while also beginning to support aging parents through healthcare decisions, housing changes, or direct financial help. In this context, it is easy to rationalize under saving for retirement: "We have to put the kids first," or "My parents sacrificed for me; I can't say no." The hard truth is that under saving today may simply shift the burden forward—your children may end up supporting you later, at precisely the stage when they are trying to support their own kids. Funding your retirement is not selfish; it is one of the most protective acts you can take for your family.

Think of retirement saving as the financial equivalent of the airplane oxygen mask rule. You secure your own mask so that you remain able to help others. In money terms, that means agreeing as a couple on a minimum retirement contribution floor—say, a combined 15% of gross income, or at least "enough to capture all employer match plus X% more"—that you treat as non negotiable in your cash flow framework. Support for parents or children then happens on top of that floor, not instead of it. Framing the conversation this way reduces guilt: "We are committing to not becoming a financial burden on our kids; within that constraint, here's what we can safely offer others." When you both accept that priority order, it becomes easier to say a bounded "yes" instead of an open ended "of course."

Helping relatives financially is healthiest when it is governed by structure rather than adrenaline. Start with your cash flow dashboard and set a specific, affordable support budget category, such as "Family Support: $300/month" or "Up to $5,000 per year for parental needs." This amount should fit after your retirement floor, emergency fund contributions, and core bills. Within that structure, prefer one time strategic assistance—paying for a critical home repair that lowers future risk, funding estate planning documents for your parents, covering a specific semester gap—over indefinite monthly transfers that quietly expand over time. When commitments will last more than a month or two, put them in writing: "We will contribute $X per month for Y months toward this expense, reviewed together in Month Z." Written terms reduce misunderstandings and make it easier to revisit when your situation changes.

Conversations with aging parents are emotionally charged because they touch identity, independence, and mortality. Approach them with curiosity and respect rather than interrogation about money. A gentle starting place is documents and decision makers: "Mom, if something happened to you suddenly, who should the doctors listen to? Where would we find your health care directive or will?" From there you can ask about key contacts, such as their attorney or financial professional, and whether anyone else knows where important papers are. Propose an "emergency binder" similar to the one you are building for your own household, framing it as a kindness to everyone rather than a power grab. When siblings are involved, have explicit discussions about caregiving roles, time expectations, and financial contributions early, before a crisis forces rushed decisions.

On the child side, the most common retirement derailing pattern is the college trap: committing to fund an expensive education at the expense of your own long term security. The trade offs are stark. Every dollar diverted from retirement in your 40s and 50s is a dollar that cannot compound for decades. Your children, by contrast, have access to loans, scholarships, work study, and the ability to choose lower cost schools. That does not mean you should not help; it means your help should be framed within the larger system. Be transparent with your teenagers about what you can and cannot do: "We will contribute $X per year, which we've built into our plan. Beyond that, we'll help you explore scholarships, in state options, and work." Your job is to balance opportunity with sustainability, not to erase every financial obstacle from your child's path. The next chapter will walk through education funding mechanics; for now, the analytical rule is simple: do not sacrifice your minimum retirement floor to fully fund college.

Stepping back, the sandwich generation reality makes a disciplined retirement plan even more important, not less. When you see retirement as a family protection plan, the choices become clearer: set and defend a baseline savings rate, build structured (not open ended) support for parents and children, and communicate expectations instead of carrying silent resentment. Combined with the gap analysis and the "enough" framework from earlier in the chapter, you now have a way to answer three critical questions together: What are we aiming at? Are we on track? And how do we help those we love without putting our own future—and theirs—at risk?

Chapter 9: College and Education Funding Without Derailing the Plan

Most parents feel it in their gut long before they put it into words: "If we don't cover college, are we setting our kids up to struggle?" The message shows up everywhere on school tours, in well meaning conversations, in glossy brochures that equate "love" with "full tuition." It's easy to internalize the idea that paying for everything is the gold standard and anything less is failure. Yet those same parents are also staring down rising mortgages, retirement timelines that feel too close, and the reality that every extra dollar has three competing jobs. This chapter is about stepping out of that anxiety loop and into leadership. You'll build an education plan that fits your actual household, not an imaginary one. Your plan will support your kids without quietly sacrificing your future stability.

As with every major money decision in this book, start by defining the goal before picking tools. The market is full of account types like 529s, custodial accounts, and taxable investing that all promise something. None of them can tell you what "supporting your child's education" should mean in your family. That is your job as a parent leader. Once you're clear on that definition, the rest of the chapter will help you translate it into specific accounts, realistic contribution targets, and simple automation so funding education becomes one integrated piece of your family wealth operating system, not a wild card that derails everything else.

Define the Education Goal Before Choosing Accounts

Before you can answer "How much do we need?" you have to answer "What are we trying to do?" Parents often skip straight to calculators and end up feeling either guilty (the number is impossibly high) or complacent (the tool says we're "on track," but we're not sure for what). The real work is values driven: deciding what role you want to play in your children's education and how that interacts with retirement, housing, debt, and your own career choices. Think of this as writing a short "education mission statement" for your family. It will not be perfect or permanent, but putting it into words creates a standard you can return to when emotions or social pressure spike.

Different families land on very different definitions of "support," and that is healthy. Some decide "fully funded" is the right target: tuition, fees, room and board for four years at a type of school they define in advance (for example, in state public, or a typical private assuming some aid). Others decide to cover a portion; possibly tuition only, a set dollar amount per year, or a capped contribution with the understanding that students will share responsibility through work, scholarships, or loans. Some focus on living expenses while expecting kids to use low cost options for tuition; others create a matching model, where for every dollar a teen contributes or earns in scholarships, the parents match it up to a limit. What matters is not which model you choose but that it lines up with your broader values (opportunity, independence, generosity, etc.) and that both partners explicitly agree. A quiet assumption—"Of course we'll pay for everything"—is one of the fastest paths to resentment and last minute financial strain.

Time horizon is the next critical variable. The age of your children and the spacing between them should heavily shape your approach. If your oldest is a toddler, you potentially have 15+ years before the first tuition bill; that longer runway means you can take more investment risk in the early years, then shift toward stability as high school approaches. If your oldest is already in middle school, you don't have the same luxury; your education savings is a medium term goal, which means relatively more emphasis on preserving capital than chasing maximum growth. Multiple children create staggered timelines: perhaps your oldest starts in eight years, the next in twelve. Instead of planning separately for each child, think in terms of a rolling 10–15 year window during which you'll be both contributing and withdrawing, and tie that combined horizon back to your overall Investment Policy Statement (IPS) or to a simple, separate "education IPS" that states your risk tolerance and investment mix for this goal.

Once you've clarified "what" and "when," you still need to confront trade offs. Education is one among several big ticket goals, and pretending it lives in its own universe is how otherwise responsible families end up underfunded for retirement or perpetually underbuilt on emergency reserves. A straightforward hierarchy helps. First, fund the non negotiables that protect the household: Tier 1 and 2 emergency reserves and core insurance. Second, ensure you're at least meeting a baseline retirement savings rate; retirement is, in effect, your children's future support plan, because under saving now can turn into dependence on them later. Only then allocate to education and other "opportunity" goals, followed by genuine extras. Making this framework explicit—"needs first, then opportunity, then extras"—helps couples resist emotional whiplash when confronted with a new college savings pitch or a relative's story about fully funding five grandkids' tuition. Documenting your chosen limits ("We will aim to cover four years at an in state public level, inflation adjusted") on your household dashboard keeps those guardrails visible and reduces the temptation to drift toward unsustainable promises.

There is one more stakeholder you should not leave out: your children. A six year old doesn't need a line by line breakdown of the family budget, but as kids grow, involving them in age appropriate ways turns education planning from a secret parental burden into a shared project that builds responsibility. For teens, seeing estimated costs for different schools, understanding the impact of scholarships or community college transfers, and discussing work expectations can dramatically reduce entitlement. When kids know, early and clearly, "Here's what we're committing to; here's what will be up to you," they are more likely to see themselves as partners rather than passive recipients. This does not mean loading them with adult anxiety; it means giving them clarity, context, and a chance to exercise agency.

With your educational "north star" defining what support means, how long you have, how it ranks among other goals, and how kids will share responsibility, you're ready to decide which tools you'll use. The next section walks through the main account types and shows how to match them to your priorities instead of chasing whatever someone at work mentioned last week.

529 Plans and Other Funding Tools: A Practical Comparison

Education funding tools are containers. Their job is to hold money, sometimes with tax advantages or special rules. They don't determine whether your plan is wise. That comes from the thinking you just did. Still, different containers can either make your life easier or create surprises, so it's worth understanding the core trade offs.

For many families, 529 plans are the logical starting point. A 529 is a tax advantaged account earmarked for qualified education expenses like tuition, mandatory fees, and often room and board when a student is enrolled sufficiently full time. You, as the parent (or another adult), typically own and control the account, even though the child is the beneficiary; they do not automatically gain control at 18. Contributions are usually made with after tax dollars, but the investment growth can be withdrawn tax free if used for qualified expenses under the relevant rules in your jurisdiction. Within a 529, you choose from a menu of investment options, often including age based portfolios that gradually shift from stocks to bonds as the beneficiary approaches college. The analytical question is: does locking money into an education specific vehicle, with tax benefits as compensation, fit your likelihood of using it for education?

Custodial accounts, often known as UGMA or UTMA accounts in the U.S. sit at a different point on the control spectrum. Technically, the assets are irrevocable gifts to the child; you manage them as the custodian until the child reaches the age of majority defined by your state, at which point legal control transfers to them. That structure can be attractive if you value flexibility in how funds are used (not just education) but still want to earmark money in the child's name. The trade offs are real: because the assets legally belong to the child, they can affect financial aid formulas and, more importantly, there is no legal mechanism to stop a 19 year old from spending inherited funds on a sports car instead of tuition. Custodial accounts may make sense for moderate sums where you want broad flexibility, supporting a mix of education, first apartment costs, or entrepreneurship but they require confidence that your future young adult will be ready for that responsibility.

A third option is simply to use a standard taxable investment account in your own names and mentally label a portion of it as the "education flexibility fund." From a control and flexibility standpoint, this is the simplest: you can invest in a wide range of assets, change your mind about how to use the money, and reassign it among children or even non education goals without penalty (aside from taxes on gains). The cost of that flexibility is the absence of specific education related tax breaks. Depending on your tax situation, the drag from taxable dividends and capital gains may be minor or material. If you highly value optionality—for example, you are not sure whether your child will attend a traditional four year program, or you want the option to redirect funds to your own retirement if circumstances demand—a taxable account can be an attractive "least regret" option, especially for savings beyond what you are confident will be used for qualified education.

Not every education dollar has to come from parental savings. Scholarships, part time work, and student contributions are core pillars of a sustainable plan. Thinking about them early allows you and your children to treat them as part of the strategy, not last minute gap fillers. Encourage your teen to see activities, grades, and essay skills as levers that can meaningfully reduce cost; many local scholarships are underapplied for simply because students never look. Reasonable work expectations during summers or lightly during the school year not only bring in cash but also build time management and responsibility. The standard you set—"We will do X; we expect you to do Y"—should align with your values: maybe you want your child to have significant "skin in the game," or perhaps you want them to focus heavily on an intense course of study while working only modestly. Either way, bringing scholarships and work into the plan keeps your savings targets realistic and reinforces the ownership mindset you began cultivating earlier.

With the tools on the table we covered like 529s, custodial accounts, taxable investing, and non savings levers you can now translate your goal into an actual number and, more importantly, a monthly habit.

A Funding Target That Keeps Life Livable

Once you start looking at projected college costs, it's easy to either freeze ("We'll never get there; why bother?") or overreact ("We have to divert everything to college now"). Both are signs that the question being asked—"What exact dollar number will we need in 10–15 years?"—is too precise for the uncertainty involved. A better approach is to choose a sustainable contribution rate that fits within your broader cash flow system, monitor it against evolving projections, and adjust over time.

Anchor on a percentage of income or a modest fixed monthly amount rather than a fantasy lump sum. You might decide that 5% of gross household income will go toward education savings once your emergency fund is in place and a baseline retirement contribution is automated. If cash is tight, begin with a flat, affordable dollar amount (say, $100 per month per child) and revisit it each year. When raises or major expense reductions occur in daycare no longer being necessary or a car loan paid off, consider intentionally increasing the education contribution rather than letting the freed up cash evaporate into lifestyle upgrades. Whatever target you choose, record it on your household dashboard alongside retirement and other priority contributions; seeing the numbers together reinforces that education is one important goal among several, not the only one that matters.

Once you've set a contribution target, automation is your best ally. Treat education savings the way you treat retirement contributions: money should move into the chosen accounts on a fixed schedule, ideally right after payday, before it has a chance to blend into daily spending. Set recurring transfers into your 529, custodial, or taxable "education flexibility" account and resist the urge to micro manage based on market headlines or college cost news. Instead, schedule a quarterly or semiannual review where you simply confirm: Are the transfers happening? Is the amount still affordable and aligned with our broader plan? Do updated projections suggest a small adjustment is warranted? This rhythm mirrors the guidance on building and maintaining other reserves in your plan. Making progress through steady systems beats heroic one off efforts.

Families with more than one child face an additional layer of complexity: how to allocate fairly. Here, "fair" does not always mean "identical." You might choose equal dollar support for each child (four years of in state tuition each), equal effort (matching whatever each child secures in scholarships or earnings), or an explicitly needs based approach if one child has special needs or a particularly costly program. The key is to choose a philosophy in advance, not in the heat of the moment when an older child is about to enroll and younger siblings are watching. From a mechanical standpoint, some parents prefer one 529 per child; others use a single family 529 and track internal "allocations." Either can work; what matters is that you can explain your system clearly and that it's documented in your family money notes so confusion and suspicion don't arise later.

You will almost certainly need to confront the "good parent" myth: the idea that loving, responsible parents should strain themselves financially to cover every possible cost so their children never have to face debt or trade offs. This belief is emotionally powerful and often reinforced by stories of families who "sacrificed everything" for education. An analytical view recognizes that there is a line between generosity and self harm. If overfunding college means underfunding your own retirement, you are not protecting your children; you are increasing the odds that they will be financially responsible for you later. If you forgo adequate insurance or emergency reserves to boost college savings, you are exposing the entire household to avoidable risk. A more durable definition of success is this: your children graduate as capable young adults who understand money, have had to exercise effort and judgment, and have access to meaningful opportunities, while you arrive at your own later years with dignity and independence. Non financial support which can include, help with applications, mentoring, emotional stability at home and networking is often more decisive for long term success than squeezing out an extra $200 per month for tuition.

If you've followed the steps in this chapter, you now have a clear definition of educational support, an understanding of the main funding tools and their trade offs, and a realistic, automated contribution plan that fits inside your larger operating system. You are not at the mercy of college inflation headlines; you are leading with intention. In the next chapter, we turn to another emotionally loaded area of family finance: housing and real estate. As with college, you will separate cultural expectations from what truly serves your family's long term stability and wealth.

Chapter 10: Real Estate and Home Decisions as Wealth Strategy

If there is one topic where emotion and numbers collide, it is housing. Your home is where your kids grow up, where you decompress after long days, and where much of your family's story unfolds. It is also likely your largest expense and one of your biggest assets. That combination makes housing decisions uniquely powerful: get them roughly right and many other pieces of your financial life become easier; get them badly wrong and even a strong income can feel chronically tight. In this chapter, we will treat your home as both shelter and strategy. Your house is something that should support your family's stability and long-term wealth, not function as a status symbol or an accidental speculative bet on a particular zip code.

We will start by examining how to right-size your housing choices, including the lure of "more house" and the pressures around school districts and neighborhoods. Then we will move into the mechanics of mortgages and refinancing, because the way you finance a home can either give your household flexibility or quietly lock you into financial rigidity. Finally, we will look at real estate as an intentional investment (rental properties and similar ventures) through a risk-aware lens. The goal is not to talk you into or out of owning more real estate, but to give you a framework so that every decision about property, primary home or investment is deliberate, aligned with your operating system, and grounded in clear trade-offs.

The House as Shelter, Not a Status Contest

One of the most powerful levers you control in your operating system is your housing cost. Yet many families treat the maximum mortgage amount the bank will approve as a recommendation rather than a warning. Lenders base approvals on income, debts, and broad guidelines, not on your actual priorities, your desire to fund college, or your hope to retire before 70. Treating the bank's upper limit as your target is like letting a car dealership decide what kind of car you "should" drive. Your family's financial resilience depends on something else entirely: how much space you genuinely need and how much cash-flow risk you are willing to accept.

The true cost of "more house" extends far beyond the monthly payment. A larger, more expensive home usually means higher property taxes, insurance, utilities, and ongoing maintenance. There are also furnishings and décor: more rooms to fill, more systems that can fail. Every extra dollar pointed at housing is a dollar that cannot go to emergency reserves, retirement, college, or debt freedom. A couple who spends $800 more per month on a house than they needed is sacrificing thousands per year in other goals, plus decades of compounding. They also need a larger emergency fund just to buffer that bigger fixed cost. Over time, a "stretch" house can convert what could have been a flexible, option-rich financial life into a paycheck-to-paycheck existence in a very nice kitchen. Choosing a smaller, more affordable home instead frees resources for other goals and often increases overall wellbeing, not just bank balances.

Beyond the spreadsheet, housing pressure shows up in relationships and careers. A high payment can make one or both spouses feel trapped in jobs they would otherwise leave or renegotiate. It can make career pivots, entrepreneurial experiments, or part-time seasons for caregiving or health feel impossible. That pressure often seeps into marital dynamics: disagreements about spending are sharper when one partner feels "we can't afford any mistakes" because the house already eats a big share of income. When you choose a home, you are not just choosing bedrooms and square footage; you are choosing how much flexibility and margin your family will have in the next decade.

For many parents, the biggest emotional driver of "more house" is school district pressure. You want your kids to have good classmates, strong teachers, and safe neighborhoods. Those are legitimate goals. The danger is when the desire for the "best" district quietly overrides commute sanity, social support, and financial sustainability. A more analytical framework helps. When comparing areas, evaluate four dimensions explicitly: safety (crime, traffic, walkability), commute (for both partners), community (friends, support, extracurriculars), and budget alignment. A slightly less "prestigious" district that still meets your standards, cuts your commute, and drops your housing cost may deliver more overall family wellbeing than the supposed top-tier option. Make the trade-offs explicit instead of letting status and fear of missing out silently drive the decision.

Home equity is another area where emotion and reality often diverge. Equity—the difference between your home's market value and the mortgage balance—is a useful component of your net worth, but it is not the same as spendable savings. It is illiquid and tied to a single asset in a single location. In a downturn, home values can stagnate or decline just when access to credit tightens. If much of your "net worth" lives in your house and you lose a job or face a health crisis, you cannot easily sell a bathroom to raise cash. You either have to borrow against the house, often on less favorable terms, or sell the entire property—an expensive, disruptive move. Treating your home like an ATM through serial cash-out refinances or frequent equity loans amplifies this risk. A more durable strategy is to build wealth across multiple asset types: retirement accounts, taxable investments, cash reserves, and home equity—but not home equity alone.

Because housing decisions are so consequential, it helps to establish a "sleep-at-night" housing rule for your family. Instead of asking, "What will the bank lend us?" ask, "What payment level lets us comfortably fund our other priorities and still breathe?" One approach is to set a ceiling on total housing costs (mortgage or rent, taxes, insurance, HOA dues) as a percentage of take-home pay that fits your cash-flow framework. Another is to run a stress test: if one income dropped by 25–50 percent for six months, could you cover your housing cost from your emergency fund and remaining income without immediately resorting to debt or desperate measures? If not, the house is too tight for your actual life. Align your housing choice with an emergency reserve designed to cover at least several months of housing costs, not just generic living expenses. The right home is one you can picture living in through a rough patch without constant panic.

Once you are looking at housing through a stability lens rather than a status lens, the question becomes: how do you structure the financing so it supports your operating system rather than undermining it?

Mortgages, Refinancing, and the Flexibility Factor

Mortgages are powerful tools. Used well, they let your family enjoy stable housing while gradually building equity. Used poorly, they can lock you into a fragile, overleveraged position.

The first major decision is mortgage term length. Shorter terms, like 15-year mortgages, typically come with lower interest rates and dramatically reduce total interest paid. However, they also require higher monthly payments. Longer terms, like 30-year mortgages, reduce the required payment, increasing cash-flow flexibility, but you pay more interest over time. The right choice is not simply "shorter is better." Instead, analyze how each option fits into your broader plan. If a 15-year term would force you to cut retirement contributions below an employer match, delay building an adequate emergency fund, or create chronic budget stress, then a 30-year term with a disciplined plan for extra principal payments may produce a stronger, more resilient household.

Refinancing decisions require similarly nuanced analysis. Many homeowners focus on the new monthly payment and the advertised interest rate, but those are only part of the story. When you refinance, you incur closing costs and often reset the loan term clock. To evaluate whether a refinance makes sense, calculate the break-even point: how many months of reduced payments it will take to recoup the closing costs. If you plan to move or significantly remodel before that break-even point, the refinance may not be worthwhile. Also examine whether you are increasing or decreasing your overall interest cost, not just your rate. If you refinance from a 30-year mortgage you have already paid for 10 years into a new 30-year loan, you may lower your monthly payment but extend your payoff date by a decade, increasing total interest unless you deliberately keep your old payment amount and treat the refinance as a way to accelerate payoff. Before signing, run through a checklist: What is the exact rate change? What are the total fees? How long do we expect to stay in this home? Will we commit to a higher payment to preserve the original payoff schedule, or are we intentionally trading time for cash flow?

Another common question is whether to make extra payments on your mortgage or invest that money instead. Mathematically, you compare the after-tax interest rate on your mortgage to the expected long-term return of your investment portfolio. If your mortgage rate is low and you reasonably expect a diversified portfolio to earn more over decades, investing appears superior in the long run. However, this ignores behavior and risk tolerance. Some people sleep far better with a paid-off home, and that peace of mind has real value. Others are comfortable carrying a low-rate mortgage indefinitely while aggressively investing. Rather than adopting an ideological stance—"always pay off the house" or "never prepay cheap debt"—build a blended policy. For example, you might commit to maxing an employer retirement match and funding your emergency reserves before sending extra to the mortgage, and then split additional surplus between extra principal and investing. The analytical question is: which allocation best supports your goals and your ability to stay the course through market ups and downs?

Home equity loans and home equity lines of credit (HELOCs) deserve particular caution. They can be useful tools when handled with clear rules, but dangerous when used casually. A fixed home equity loan provides a lump sum with a fixed repayment schedule; a HELOC functions more like a credit card secured by your house, with a revolving line you can draw on and repay. In both cases, you are turning home equity into new debt. To keep this from eroding your wealth, only use such borrowing for defined, high-priority purposes with a specific repayment plan—for example, a necessary major repair, a carefully budgeted renovation that truly enhances the home's value and your quality of life, or consolidating higher-rate debt with the firm intention to pay it off and close the line. Avoid using home equity as a substitute for an emergency fund or for lifestyle upgrades that could have been deferred. Any time you borrow against your house, document the decision in your family money notes: why you are borrowing, how much, how you will repay it, and what changes if circumstances shift. That simple act increases accountability and reduces the risk of slow, unnoticed equity leakage.

With your primary home right-sized and your mortgage supporting rather than constraining your operating system, you may at some point wonder about owning additional properties.

Real Estate Investing: A Risk-Aware Family Framework

Before your household considers real estate investing, examine readiness on three fronts: financial, protection, and time capacity. Financially, you should have stable emergency reserves that cover both personal and property-specific risks, a solid insurance foundation (including adequate liability and possibly umbrella coverage), and a clear retirement savings plan already in motion. Using savings meant for your own emergency fund or halting retirement contributions to scramble into a rental property is usually a red flag. Protection-wise, understand how an additional property changes your risk profile: landlord liability, property damage, and local regulatory environment all matter. Finally, evaluate your time capacity. Even with a property manager, real estate demands decisions, oversight, and bandwidth. If both partners are already at or beyond capacity, adding a rental can become a chronic source of stress rather than an asset.

When analyzing a potential investment property, focus first on cash flow, not just hoped-for appreciation. Appreciation is uncertain and largely outside your control. Cash flow is the relationship between rent collected and all expenses: mortgage principal and interest, taxes, insurance, maintenance, repairs, vacancy periods, property management fees, and reserves for capital expenditures like roofs and HVAC systems. Rental income that barely covers the mortgage but ignores these other costs is not positive cash flow; it is a fragile bet that nothing will go wrong. Build conservative pro formas: assume some vacancy each year, overestimate maintenance, and include a monthly reserve for major future repairs. If the numbers only work under best-case scenarios, the risk to your family's stability may be too high. A modest but reliably positive cash flow, on the other hand, can contribute to resilience by diversifying income sources and helping to service its own risks.

Concentration risk is another key consideration. Real estate is lumpy. A single property can represent a large percentage of your net worth, and its performance is tied to one local economy, one set of regulations, and a small number of tenants. If that neighborhood declines, or if you experience a long vacancy or an expensive legal dispute, the impact can be significant. As your net worth grows, set a household cap on how much of it you are comfortable concentrating in any one property or even in real estate as an asset class. That cap might be, for example, no more than 50 percent of net worth in all real estate, or no more than 20 percent in any one investment property, depending on your risk tolerance and time horizon. Maintaining diversification across stocks, bonds, cash, and real estate helps prevent one local shock from endangering your entire operating system.

Because real estate decisions are often emotionally charged—driven by fear of missing out, enthusiasm for a particular house, or persuasive stories from friends—impose a discipline of written decision documentation. Before you commit to an investment property, create a one-page investment summary that includes: purchase price, expected rents, all estimated expenses, financing terms, expected cash flow under conservative assumptions, vacancy and repair allowances, your downside scenario, and your exit options. Specify your criteria for success over the first 12–24 months and what would prompt you to sell, refinance, or change strategy. Review this summary together as spouses, and do not proceed until both partners are genuinely aligned.

Once you own the property, schedule an annual performance review: compare actual income and expenses to your original assumptions, reassess risks, and confirm that the investment still fits your overall family plan.

Real estate can be part of a thoughtful family wealth strategy, but only when it sits on top of a solid foundation: right-sized primary housing, healthy cash flow, appropriate insurance, and a clear investing policy that includes other asset classes. In the next chapter, we will look at another major engine of family wealth—your income itself. Just as housing decisions can either constrain or expand your options, how you pursue raises, promotions, and side streams of income will influence the speed and safety with which your family moves toward its goals.

Chapter 11: Income Growth and Side Streams Without Chaos

Most money books talk almost entirely about cutting back. Skip the latte. Clip the coupons. Cancel the kids' activities. For a lot of middle- and upper-middle–income families, that advice feels insulting and, frankly, impossible. You're already running hot: two careers, pickups and drop-offs, homework, aging parents, maybe a side role in your community or faith group. There is not some giant ball of frivolous spending to "trim" without real pain. What usually moves the needle in this season is not extreme frugality, but thoughtful income growth which needs to be handled in a way that doesn't blow up your marriage, your health, or your kids' sense of having parents who are actually present.

In this chapter, you'll treat income strategy as part of your role as a family wealth leader. You'll see how modest increases in income, captured by a simple system, can accelerate almost every goal in this book: emergency buffers, debt paydown, retirement, college, and generosity. You'll also see the other side: how chasing "more" without guardrails turns into burnout, resentment, and projects that quietly lose money. We'll move step by step, from strengthening the income you already have, to negotiating for more, to adding side streams and possible business ownership, while keeping your core family operating system safe.

The Income Ladder: Grow the Engine First

Most families know more income would help; fewer see how it fits into the broader wealth equation. Mathematically, family wealth is built by three variables working together: income, savings rate, and time. For busy households that already have a reasonable handle on spending, increasing income—even by 5–10%—can fund multiple priorities simultaneously if you capture it deliberately. An $7,000 after-tax raise might mean $3,000 more toward retirement, $2,000 to college savings, and $2,000 to faster debt payoff every year. Over a decade, with growth, that's the difference between "we hope this works" and "we can see the numbers lining up."

The risk is lifestyle inflation is letting every raise quietly turn into a nicer car, more takeout, or a bigger house payment. Without a system, higher income just raises the stakes of your stress instead of reducing it. That's why income strategy belongs next to dashboards and automation, not off in its own motivational silo. When you treat income as one lever in an integrated plan, you stop asking, "Should I hustle more?" and start asking, "If we earn an extra $500 a month, exactly what problem will it solve, and what rules will keep it from disappearing?" The opportunity cost of more work is real: time, presence, energy, and mental bandwidth. Income growth should be judged not just by the dollars, but by the net improvement in family resilience and well-being.

Seen this way, your career is not only a paycheck; it is a risk-management asset. Skill-building, strong relationships, and professional reputation increase your "employability," which is the real hedge against layoffs, industry shifts, or the need to move for family reasons. A practical tool here is a "career runway" plan: once a year, you deliberately update your résumé, list key accomplishments, refresh professional profiles, and note concrete skills or certifications that would noticeably improve your options over the next 3–5 years. Maintain a short list of people to stay in touch with—former managers, mentors, colleagues who know your work. This isn't about constant job-hopping; it is about never letting your ability to generate income become a single, brittle point of failure. A healthy runway plan also connects to your emergency fund strategy: if your skills are current and your network is active, you may need fewer months of ultra-defensive cash than someone whose prospects would take longer to rebuild.

In two-income households, it's tempting to think of both incomes as "equal." They rarely are, when you look under the hood. One job might carry the health benefits, retirement match, and more predictable hours; the other might be more flexible but easier to replace. For planning, it is useful to define a "primary" income, not as a value statement about either partner, but as an analytical classification based on three factors: total dollars, attached benefits, and how necessary that income is to maintain your minimum lifestyle. The primary income is the one that, if lost, would most stress your cash flow; it's also the first place to focus disability coverage, job-security conversations, and targeted skill investment. The secondary income may be the better candidate for experimentation, reduced hours, a job change, a career pivot, but it still deserves a contingency plan. What happens if either income disappears for six months? Your household operating system should make that an explicit scenario, not an unspoken fear.

All of this sits inside one hard constraint: time. Time is a family asset, not an infinite backdrop. Every additional shift, side project, or late-night email has a cost somewhere: on sleep, patience with your kids, or your ability to make good decisions. One of the clearest signs that an income strategy is misaligned is when your evenings and weekends become "spillover zones" with no boundaries and everyone in the house feels it. To prevent this, adopt a simple rule: any income-growth plan must include explicit time limits before it's approved. For example, "I'll work one extra evening a week and Saturday morning for the next 12 weeks, then we will evaluate," rather than "I'll just grind for a while." Use your existing family finance meeting to check in on capacity at least quarterly. Are you both sleeping? Is anyone resentful? Is the financial benefit worth the strain? When you normalize these questions, you send a clear signal: money is important, but not more important than health and relationships.

Once you've framed income growth as part of a broader, system-based plan, the next step is obvious: make the income you already have work harder by getting paid closer to what you're worth and then capturing those gains.

Raises, Promotions, and the "Raise Capture" System

In many families, major income gains are hidden in plain sight: within your current job. But asking for more money or a promotion feels intimidating, so years go by with pay that lags behind contribution. To approach this analytically, you need evidence and a plan, not wishful thinking.

Start by preparing a one-page value case. List your measurable outcomes (revenue influenced, costs reduced, projects delivered), the responsibilities you've taken on beyond your original job description, and any skills or certifications you've added. Include brief supporting data where possible: before-and-after metrics, client feedback, or internal performance reviews. This forces you to see your role through your employer's lens: where have you created value the organization cares about?

Alongside that value case, gather reasonable market context like salary ranges for similar roles, internal job postings at higher levels, or guidelines published by HR. Then define two numbers: your target (what you believe is fair given your contribution and market), and your minimum acceptable outcome (which might be a smaller raise paired with a concrete path to more responsibility). Going into the conversation with these anchors protects you from being derailed by nerves.

When you sit down with your manager, remember that "compensation" is broader than base salary. It includes bonuses, restricted stock units (RSUs), retirement match, health insurance, paid leave, flexible scheduling, training budgets, and remote-work options. In some seasons of family life, an extra day at home each week or a stronger 401(k) match may be worth more than a modest salary bump. Enter the discussion ready to explore this whole menu. You might ask: "If budget for base salary is tight this year, are there other levers? Possibly a bonus structure, match, learning budget, or flexibility that we can adjust?" Whatever the outcome, tie your requests back to the value you provide, not to personal need: "Here's the additional scope I've taken on and the results we've achieved; I'd like my compensation structure to reflect that level of contribution."

Negotiating more income is only half of the equation. The other half is what happens to that money on payday. Without a system, higher pay quickly disappears into lifestyle creep. This is where the Raise Capture Rule comes in. Before any raise hits your account, you and your partner decide, in writing, what percentage of future raises will be automatically redirected to long-term priorities. For example: "We will route 70% of any net raise to retirement and college savings and keep 30% for lifestyle." Implement that rule through your payroll system or bank automation the moment a raise is confirmed. This structure lets you enjoy some immediate improvement such as nicer date nights or better travel without sacrificing the compounding power of higher savings. Over a decade, consistent raise capture can meaningfully increase retirement contributions without feeling like a sacrifice, because the increased saving comes from money you didn't have before.

Even with these structures, you need a disciplined way to ensure that the career and compensation path you're on still makes sense. A quarterly check-in is a simple tool for this. Once every three months, use your family meeting to evaluate the tradeoffs of current work: How many hours are you each actually working? How stressed do you feel, on a 1–10 scale? Has your net financial position grown in line with the extra effort? If the answer is "we're exhausted and the numbers aren't moving," that's a signal to reconsider: perhaps a different role, a boundary around after-hours communication, or shifting effort from overtime in the main job to a more lucrative or satisfying side project. If the additional push has clearly accelerated debt payoff or retirement funding, you can consciously choose to maintain it for another season. The key is to prevent "just one more busy quarter" from becoming your permanent operating mode.

For some households, the next rung on the income ladder is not more from the primary job, but an additional income stream. Done poorly, side hustles drain time and money. Done well, they add resilience and speed your progress toward key goals. The difference lies in the guardrails.

Side Income and Business Ownership: Guardrails First

The internet is full of endless lists of "best side hustles" and "easy businesses you can start this weekend." You don't need hype; you need a framework. A good side income for a family has three characteristics: it fits your real time constraints, it leverages skills you already have (so ramp-up is quick), and it aligns with your financial priorities instead of competing with them. That might look like a professional using their expertise for limited consulting hours, a parent doing remote freelance work, or a couple turning a hobby into a small, testable product.

Before you pick a tactic, clarify your goal. Are you trying to generate an extra $300 a month to accelerate debt payoff? Build a business that might one day replace your job? Or simply create a flexible stream that gives you more autonomy over time? The answer should drive which ideas even make it onto your list. Given your goal and time budget, compare broad categories: freelancing or consulting; e-commerce (products you create or resell); teaching or coaching; and asset-based approaches like renting out part of your home or equipment. For busy parents, side hustles you can do from home often make the most sense, because they reduce commuting friction and can be slotted into predictable windows.

Start with the lowest-cost experiment that plausibly fits your skills: one test client, one small batch of product, or a short course you pilot with a handful of students. Avoid ideas that require large upfront capital or long lead times before you see any cash flow; those belong, if at all, in a later chapter of your financial life when your core systems are already robust.

From day one, keep the money separate. Open a dedicated checking account for your side or business activity. All income goes in there; all expenses come out. This boundary clarifies whether the activity is actually profitable, simplifies bookkeeping and taxes, protects your main household account from accidental overdrafts, and reduces emotional arguments about "whose" money is being spent on what. Agree on a profit allocation rule before the first dollar arrives. For example: 30% of profit reserved for taxes, 20% reinvested in the side business (tools, education, marketing), and 50% transferred into your household account to be deployed according to your existing funding waterfall. When you treat side income as part of the operating system rather than "extra" money, you're far less likely to let it evaporate into random consumption.

Taxes and insurance are two areas where side income can introduce risk if neglected. Even relatively small freelance or business income is usually taxable. If no one is withholding on your behalf, you may need to set aside money for estimated quarterly tax payments and maintain basic records: invoices, receipts, mileage logs if relevant. At a minimum, use your dedicated account as a paper trail and avoid mixing personal and business charges. On the insurance side, certain activities like home-based childcare, consulting in regulated fields, or selling physical products may require or benefit from added coverage. This might be a rider on your existing homeowners policy, a small business liability policy, or professional indemnity coverage, depending on what you do. As a rule, any time your work could plausibly cause financial harm to others, ask an insurance professional what protection is appropriate. If the side venture grows into a meaningful asset, loop your estate plan in as well: who owns the business, what happens to it if you're incapacitated, and how its value will transfer.

Finally, define success and exit criteria upfront. Too many families endure years of a side business that never really makes money, but no one feels permitted to question it because "we've already invested so much." You can prevent this with a 90-day experiment frame. Before starting, you and your partner answer four questions: How much time per week will this take, and when will that time come from? How much cash are we willing to invest in the test? What metrics will define success (revenue, profit, or validated demand)? And under what conditions will we pause, pivot, or stop? At the end of 90 days, evaluate honestly. If the project is generating meaningful profit and still fits within your family's time and energy limits, renew the experiment for another season, perhaps with slightly expanded goals. If it's losing money or creating too much stress, close it down and redirect that time back into rest, family, or other income strategies.

Throughout, keep one principle in view: the purpose of additional income is to provide for your family with purpose and peace, not to prove your worth. A well-chosen side income or business can be a powerful tool, but only if it sits inside a clear operating system. It has to be one that protects your core financial stability, your marriage, and the kind of home life you're trying to build. In the next chapter, we'll take that same risk-aware lens and apply it to the rest of your protection layer: property, liability, and identity, so that the wealth you're working so hard to create isn't one bad day away from being wiped out.

Chapter 12: Protect the Household: Liability, Property, and Identity

The moment you begin to build real wealth, your household quietly becomes a more attractive target for lawsuits, for accidents that exceed basic insurance limits, and for criminals who would happily use your identity as a gateway into your accounts. None of these risks look dramatic day to day. You drive the kids to practice, host friends for a barbecue, pay your bills online, and everything feels normal. Yet a single car accident with serious injuries, a guest falling on your front steps, or a thief taking over your email and draining your bank accounts can undo years of steady progress. This chapter is about building a protective shell around the operating system you've created, so that one bad day doesn't become a multi-year financial setback.

Up to this point, you've focused on protecting income, organizing cash flow, and building assets. Here, the focus shifts to defending the balance sheet and the infrastructure that supports it. That means thinking beyond "Do I have life insurance?" into broader questions: "If someone sues us, what's really at risk?" "If our house is damaged, could we afford to repair or replace it without sabotaging retirement?" "If someone got into my email, how hard would it be for them to impersonate me financially?" None of these topics are fun, but they are squarely in the realm of family leadership. Thoughtful preparation turns frightening hypotheticals into manageable, contained events.

The Risk Map Beyond Life Insurance

As families build assets such as home equity, retirement accounts, and growing savings they unintentionally raise their profile in ways that most people never consider. Liability is not an abstract legal term; it's the gap between the harm someone says you caused and what your existing insurance is willing to pay. If that gap is large, your savings and investments are effectively exposed.

Liability is a net-worth issue because the more you own, the more someone can plausibly seek in a lawsuit. Picture a car accident where you're at fault and multiple people are injured, or a teenager in your household posts something online that another family claims is defamatory. Even if you ultimately prevail, defending yourself costs money; if you lose, a judgment can reach beyond the liability limits on your auto or homeowners policy. Everyday scenarios—your dog biting a visitor, a contractor getting hurt on your property, an accidental kitchen fire that spreads to a neighbor's unit—are the raw material for claims. Recognizing that your wealth makes you more visible does not mean living in fear; it means acknowledging that part of peace of mind is making sure your legal and insurance structure is proportionate to your balance sheet.

Home and auto coverage are often treated as commodities: people shop by premium, glance at the declarations page, and then file the policy away. The fine print, however, determines how much protection you actually have. Basic components include liability limits (how much the policy will pay if you're responsible for injuries or damage), deductibles (how much you pay out of pocket before coverage kicks in), and how property is valued (actual cash value vs. replacement cost). Minimum state auto limits or rock-bottom home coverage might look affordable, but in a serious event they can force you to liquidate investments or take on debt to make up the difference. Underinsuring is effectively self-insuring the gap with your own wealth. Periodic review, especially at renewals or after life changes like buying a new car, renovating, or adding a teen driver keeps the protection layer aligned with your current reality rather than with the starter policy you bought years ago.

In a digital world, identity theft and account takeover are no longer fringe risks. They are central threats to any family's financial system. Attackers don't need to break into your house; they need to trick you or your systems. Phishing emails mimic legitimate institutions and coax you into revealing logins. Reused passwords across sites allow one breach to unlock multiple doors. SIM swaps, where a criminal convinces a phone provider to move your number to their device can defeat text-based authentication, giving them access to banking and email. When those channels are compromised, your payroll deposit, savings, and credit lines become vulnerable. Modern wealth management must therefore include basic cyber hygiene as deliberately as it includes budgeting or investing. Establishing household security standards of what's acceptable, what's non-negotiable reduces the space for error.

Disaster readiness is also financial readiness. A house fire, flood, regional storm, or extended power outage is not just a logistical hassle; it's a stress test of your entire operating system. Do you have recent backups of essential documents and data? Could you quickly access cash for temporary housing, food, and transportation? Are critical phone numbers and accounts accessible if your devices are lost or destroyed? Preparedness basics like scanning key documents into secure storage, keeping copies of IDs and policies, maintaining updated emergency contacts translate directly into faster recovery and fewer irreversible financial choices made under pressure. The emergency binder you assembled earlier is the backbone here; disaster planning is about ensuring that binder is findable, usable, and complemented by adequate insurance.

When you step back, you can see your risk map expanding: beyond "Will my family be okay if I die?" to "What if someone sues us, impersonates us, or we can't live in our home for three months?" That broader view positions you to take concrete, manageable action.

A Protection Checklist You Can Complete This Month

Awareness without action only amplifies anxiety. The goal of this section is not to turn you into an insurance expert, but to give you a short, prioritized checklist you can realistically work through in one or two money sessions. Think of it as a tune-up for the protective shell around your family wealth.

Start with a 30-minute policy review. Pull the declarations pages for your home (or renters) and auto policies with summary sheets that show key coverages and limits. You don't need to digest every clause; focus on a small set of numbers: bodily injury liability limits, property damage limits, personal liability on your home policy, deductibles, and any special riders (for jewelry, home business, etc.). Record these figures and your renewal dates on your family dashboard so they live alongside your other critical data. As you review, write down at least one question for each policy to discuss with your insurer or agent—for example, "How would this policy respond if a guest is seriously injured on our property?" or "What would it cost to increase liability limits from X to Y?" This brief exercise converts a vague sense of "we're probably covered" into a clearer understanding of what you actually have.

For many households with rising assets, an umbrella liability policy is the most cost-effective additional layer of defense. Umbrella coverage sits on top of your home and auto policies, increasing your liability protection once those primary limits are exhausted. In practical terms, if you are sued for an amount greater than your auto policy's liability limit, the umbrella can cover the excess up to its own limit, within policy terms. Typical triggers for considering an umbrella include higher income, significant savings or investments, owning a home, having teen drivers, or owning rental property. Because umbrella policies are designed to handle low-probability, high-severity events, the additional coverage per dollar of premium is often relatively inexpensive compared with the potential downside. The objective is alignment: your umbrella limit should reflect both your current net worth and the realistic scale of claims that could arise from your lifestyle.

Next, coordinate deductibles with your cash reserves. A higher deductible usually means a lower premium, effectively shifting more of the "first dollars" of a loss back onto you. That can be smart if you have a robust Tier 1 emergency buffer and are comfortable self-funding minor events. It is dangerous if a single deductible would force you into credit card debt. Review deductibles on home and auto in light of your emergency fund design: if your Tier 1 cash is, for example, one month of essential expenses, a deductible that consumes half of that might be excessive. Document your deductible strategy in your family money notes: why you chose each level, how you'll fund it if needed, and under what conditions you would revisit the choice. This transforms deductibles from arbitrary numbers into deliberate components of your risk plan.

Finally, institutionalize an annual renewal ritual. During your yearly family wealth reset, include a protection segment. Ask three simple questions: What has changed in our lives since last year? Do our coverage amounts and types still match our assets and risks? Are we clear on who to call and what to do in an emergency? Use that meeting to review any new cars, renovations, drivers, or home-based business activities and confirm they're disclosed to your insurer. Verify that contact information and beneficiaries on relevant policies are up to date. Over time, this ritual cures the "set it and forget it" problem; your protection layer becomes a living system that adapts as your life evolves.

With your property and liability coverage brought up to speed, the next frontier is the digital layer. The set of practices that keep your financial operating system from being compromised via your devices and accounts.

Family Cyber Hygiene: Simple Rules, Big Protection

Your household already has informal technology habits based off of how you choose passwords, where you store logins, whether you click links in emails. Cyber hygiene is about making those habits explicit, intentional, and aligned with the value of what you're protecting. You do not need a technical background to materially reduce your risk; you need a small set of clear rules everyone in the family can understand and follow.

The foundation is a password manager and strong two-factor authentication. A password manager allows you to generate and store unique, complex passwords for each account without needing to memorize them all. This directly addresses one of the core recommendations from consumer protection authorities: avoid reusing passwords and safeguard them instead of keeping them in browsers or on paper. Start by putting your highest-value accounts—banking, investment, email, cloud storage—into the manager. Then enable two-factor authentication (2FA) on those same accounts, preferring app-based codes or hardware keys over text messages when possible. This creates two hurdles for an attacker: something they know (your password) and something they have (your device or token). Finally, build a shared emergency access plan between spouses: store the master password and recovery details in your emergency binder or other secure location so either partner can access critical accounts if the other is unavailable.

Your email account deserves special treatment because it is the master key for most password resets. If an attacker controls your primary email, they can often reset logins for banks, investment platforms, and retailers. Protect this account with your strongest available authentication and carefully chosen recovery options. Review backup email addresses and phone numbers associated with the account; outdated or compromised recovery paths can become back doors. Some families choose to separate financial life from casual sign-ups by using one email address only for banking, taxes, and government communication, and another for newsletters, shopping, and app registrations. This segmentation doesn't guarantee safety, but it narrows the attack surface and helps you monitor important messages more reliably.

Next, consider credit monitoring and credit freezing as tools for defending your identity on the financial side. Monitoring services alert you when new accounts are opened or certain changes occur on your credit report. They are helpful for early detection but do not by themselves prevent fraudulent accounts. A credit freeze, by contrast, restricts new creditors from accessing your report, making it harder for identity thieves to open accounts in your name without lifting the freeze. For many families, especially those not frequently applying for new credit, a freeze is an efficient default: you temporarily thaw it when genuinely needed. Document whichever approach you choose; monitoring only, freezing, or a combination in your emergency binder, along with instructions for how to lift or modify settings. This ensures that in the stressful aftermath of a suspected breach, you aren't scrambling to remember which bureau you contacted or what credentials you used.

Finally, extend cyber hygiene to kids and their devices. Children are often enthusiastic adopters of technology but lack the instinctive skepticism that comes with adult experience. Teaching them basic scam awareness about not clicking unknown links, don't share passwords with friends, be cautious about in-app prompts is a form of future identity protection. Set clear household rules for app purchases, in-game spending, and the use of shared devices linked to family payment methods. Explain, in age-appropriate language, that someone misusing their account can cause real financial harm to the family. Early habits such as creating proper logins, logging out of shared devices, and asking before entering personal information lay the groundwork for responsible financial identity management later in life.

Taken together, these practices turn your digital environment from a loosely guarded doorway into a reasonably fortified entrance. You will never eliminate all risk—that's not the goal. The goal is to make your household a significantly harder target than the average user, and to ensure that if something does go wrong, you catch it early and have the tools to respond.

A well-protected household is not just one with insurance policies on a shelf. It is a family that understands its risk map, uses coverage and cash reserves intentionally, and treats digital security as part of financial stewardship. As you strengthen these layers regarding liability, property, and identity, you are not being paranoid. You are honoring the effort you've invested in building your family's wealth operating system. With this protective shell in place, you are better positioned to turn your attention to the next dimension of your legacy: raising children who are equipped to handle money, responsibility, and opportunity without entitlement. That is where we turn next.

Chapter 13: Teaching Kids About Money Without Raising Entitlement

Most parents I meet are carrying a quiet paradox: they are working incredibly hard to create stability and opportunity for their kids and at the same time, they're a little afraid that generosity will backfire. They worry about raising children who feel entitled to comfort they didn't earn, or who arrive at adulthood without the skills to manage what the family has built. Underneath the college savings accounts, the birthday money, and the travel sports fees is a deeper question: "How do we give our kids enough without accidentally giving them too much?"

This chapter treats that question as a leadership challenge, not a moral indictment. You cannot guarantee that your children will "turn out" a certain way. You can, however, design a family system that steadily builds competence: the ability to understand money, make decisions, live within limits, handle mistakes, and connect money to values rather than ego. The goal is not perfection; it is progressive readiness. You will see how to layer skills over time, from a preschooler dropping coins into a jar to a 17 year old understanding paychecks and car insurance so that by the time real dollars and real stakes show up, your kids already have a framework. And you will do it in a way that fits real life: short conversations, simple structures, and rituals you can sustain when you are tired.

The Goal: Competence, Not Perfection

When you imagine your child at 25, "financially ready" probably does not mean that they never make a questionable purchase, or that they can recite tax code. It looks more like this: they can distinguish wants from needs; delay gratification when it matters; use tools like credit and debit without spiraling into debt; understand that money is linked to work, priorities, and trade-offs; and know that when they make a mistake, the response is to adjust the plan, not to hide in shame. That level of competence is not an innate trait. It is the result of hundreds of small experiences, guided by you.

The most powerful way to shape those experiences is to begin with values, not with numbers. Before you decide whether to pay for an allowance, or how much to contribute to a first car, clarify what you are trying to teach. Many families land on a short list: generosity, discipline, responsibility, gratitude. Those words are too abstract to teach on their own, so you translate them into observable behaviors. Generosity might mean that a portion of any money a child receives is directed to causes or people they care about. Discipline might mean following through on a savings goal before spending on something impulsive. Responsibility might show up as following through on a shift at work even when social plans appear. Gratitude might mean acknowledging that certain opportunities like lessons, trips, and gifts are not guaranteed. When you are unsure how to respond to a money request, these values become your compass.

None of this works if it is just talk. Children are exquisitely sensitive to hypocrisy. If you tell them that "debt is dangerous" but routinely swipe a card for unplanned purchases and complain about the statement later, they will absorb your behavior far more than your words. Modeling does not require perfection, but it does require transparency: "We bought more than we planned this month, and I don't like how that feels. Here's what I'm going to change." That honesty communicates that adults also have to align money with values and that course corrections are normal.

Competence emerges in stages. In the early years, roughly ages 3 to 7, children can grasp that money is used to get things, that different things cost different amounts, and that you sometimes have to wait. Simple saving jars or a clear piggy bank, pretending to play "store," and counting coins lay tracks for concepts like budgeting and trade-offs. Helping a six year old wait three weeks to buy a toy is a direct exercise in delayed gratification, a capacity linked to later social and academic success. You are not only teaching about money; you are building self control.

In the "middle years," roughly 8 to 12, kids can begin setting simple goals, comparing prices, and understanding that money is finite. This is where an allowance or earnings from age appropriate tasks can become a laboratory: "You get this much each week; here's how long it will take to reach that game if you save half." They are ready to see that choices today affect options later. In the teen years, complexity expands: bank accounts, part time jobs, digital payments, subscriptions, and social pressure. Here, your role shifts from traffic cop to coach. Instead of dictating every decision, you help them analyze: "If you put $200 toward this car upgrade, what happens to your plan for prom or summer?"

You also want mistakes to appear early, when the stakes are low. A ten year old who blows their entire "spend" jar on a flimsy toy and then has to wait several weeks to rebuild learns something visceral about impulse purchases that no lecture can match. Your instinct may be to rescue: to "spot them" the money so they do not feel disappointed. Over time, that undermines competence. A more productive stance is to let the natural consequence stand, then debrief: "You seem frustrated. What did you learn from how you spent your money? What might you do differently next time?" The goal is to frame mistakes as curriculum, not character flaws.

At the same time, you need to calibrate transparency so you are not handing your children your adult fears. "We're making a budget so we can afford the vacation and still save for retirement" is useful; "I don't know how we're going to pay the mortgage next month" is terrifying. Let your kids see that adults plan, prioritize, and sometimes say no to themselves. Invite them into simplified versions of your family money meetings: "Tonight we're deciding which activities we can afford next season. Here's the total we've set aside, and here are the options." Over years, that exposure communicates that money is a tool for living out values and caring for one another, not a measure of worth.

Once you have that philosophical backbone of values, milestones, tolerance for mistakes, appropriate transparency, you are ready to embed it in daily routines. The most powerful tools are often the simplest: how you structure allowance, how you talk about chores, and how you handle everyday purchases.

Allowances, Chores, and the Earning Mindset

Allowance is one of the most emotionally loaded topics in family finance. Parents worry that "paying for chores" will breed entitlement, or that "giving money for nothing" will disconnect money from effort. There is no single correct model, but there are three primary patterns, each aligned with different values and each workable if used intentionally.

A no strings allowance treats money as a learning tool, not a wage. You give a fixed amount at regular intervals. You can start with weekly for younger children, maybe monthly as they age, simply because they are part of the family. Core chores (making the bed, clearing dishes, basic tidying) are expected contributions, not tied to pay. The purpose of the allowance is to practice budgeting, saving, and giving. This approach emphasizes that being in a family comes with both rights (support) and responsibilities (helping).

A chore tied allowance connects money directly to work. Kids are paid for specific tasks completed, and no work means no pay. This can build a strong link between effort and income but brings risk: children may begin to treat every request for help as a transaction. If you choose this model, be explicit about which chores are simply part of living in the household and which are optional, paid work. A hybrid model often works best: baseline chores that are non negotiable and unpaid, plus an "extra work board" with clearly priced tasks such as washing the car, deep cleaning a bathroom, or yard work, that children can choose to earn extra. This lets you cultivate both contribution and entrepreneurship.

Whatever model you choose, consistency matters more than the exact dollar amount. An age based guideline such as giving a child weekly allowance equal to half their age or their full age in dollars provides a simple formula and creates a rationale for "raises" as children grow. There is no magic number; your budget and comfort level set the ceiling. A better question than "What is the right amount?" is "Is this enough to make decisions meaningful, without being so large that mistakes become costly?"

Once money is flowing, you need a simple structure to teach allocation. A three bucket or "three jars" system of Spend, Save, Donate, is effective because it is concrete. At each allowance payout, your child decides how much goes into each container. The Spend jar funds short term wants. If the desired item costs more than is currently in the jar, they can either wait and accumulate or choose something else. The Save jar is attached to a specific goal; write the target (a LEGO set, a special outing) on the front and let your child experience the satisfaction of watching the total move closer. The Donate jar introduces the idea that part of our money is meant to benefit others. Let your child choose causes that matter to them so generosity feels personal, not coercive.

Notice that allowance and chores are serving two different curricula. Chores teach contribution, responsibility, and cooperation. Money teaches planning, choice, and consequence. Keeping them conceptually distinct makes your life easier. You can say, "You are expected to clear the table because you live here, not because I pay you. If you'd like to earn extra for that bigger goal, here are three optional tasks." Over time, this clarity becomes part of your children's internal script about work and money.

Every purchase, no matter how small, is a chance to reinforce those scripts. When your child wants something in a store, resist the reflexive "We can't afford that" unless it is strictly true. Instead, frame the decision. "You have $15 in your Spend jar. This toy costs $12. If you buy it, you'll have $3 left. You've also been talking about saving for that larger item. What's more important to you right now?" This language respects your child's agency, reminds them of their goals, and demonstrates that money decisions are about priorities, not just price.

Waiting is a powerful muscle to build. You might institute a simple rule: for non essential purchases above a certain amount, we wait 24 hours. If your child still wants the item after a day, you revisit the choice. In the age of one click shopping, this tiny speed bump cultivates reflection. You can also start conversations about quality versus price: "We can buy this cheaper version now, which might break soon, or save longer for the one that will last. What do you think?" You are helping your children build an internal dialogue they will someday use without you present.

As kids grow, the numbers get larger and the context expands. The principles remain the same. Adolescence is your best window to practice adult sized decisions while you are still close enough to catch them.

Teens and Young Adults: Credit, Cars, and Real World Costs

By the early teen years, your child's financial world typically includes digital payments, peer pressure around clothes and experiences, and the looming reality of cars, college, and eventual independence. Your task is to equip them with a clear understanding of the tools they will encounter—credit, bank accounts, insurance, taxes—without either sugarcoating or catastrophizing.

Credit is a prime example. Many young adults' first serious money mistake involves a credit card. You can reduce that risk by demystifying credit long before a card offer arrives. Explain that a credit score is essentially a "trust score" that lenders and landlords use to judge how reliably someone pays back borrowed money. The exact formula is complex, but the key drivers are simple: pay on time, avoid carrying high balances relative to your limit, and keep accounts in good standing over time. Emphasize that a credit card is not free money; it is a short term loan. Paying the statement in full every month is responsible use. Paying only the minimum and letting a balance ride is expensive because interest accumulates.

If you choose to add a teen as an authorized user on your card to build their credit history, set explicit family rules: what, if anything, may they charge? How will they track their spending? Under what conditions would you remove the card? Sit down monthly and review the statement together, pointing out interest, due dates, and how charges map back to decisions. This is more instructive than lecturing about "being careful."

Cars are another arena where entitlement can quietly grow. Vehicles carry glamour for teens and substantial ongoing costs for families. When you talk about cars, talk in total cost, not just purchase price. Use real numbers where possible: "If the car payment is $250 per month, insurance for a teen driver is $150, gas is about $80, and we should set aside $50 a month for maintenance, that's $530 every month. Where will that come from?" Then, clarify expectations. Will the teen contribute from a part time job? Are you willing to fund a basic, safe car but not upgrades? Do grades or safe driving behaviors affect your contributions? Writing these understandings down. You can literally make this a one page agreement. Documenting these expectations reduces future conflict and makes the boundaries feel fair rather than arbitrary.

Work, even in modest amounts, is one of the best teachers available. A part time job, summer work, or structured gigs give teens direct experience with effort, time, and pay. When your child earns their first paycheck, sit down together and decode it. Point out gross pay versus net pay. Explain why taxes and other deductions exist in concept. Ask your teen to choose a percentage of each paycheck to save and a percentage they are free to spend, then help them set up simple systems so that decision is executed consistently. You are reinforcing that "pay yourself first" is a habit.

As teens edge toward college or other post high school paths, your family's expectations and boundaries matter as much as the numbers. Ambiguity is fertile ground for entitlement. One of the most protective conversations you can have is also one of the most uncomfortable: "Here is what we, as parents, are willing and able to pay for. Here is what will be your responsibility." That might include how much, if anything, you contribute toward tuition, whether you will fund a car or only insurance, whether you will pay phone bills, and under what conditions your support would change.

For older teens, write these agreements down and treat them seriously. This is not about turning your home into a contract negotiation; it is about bringing clarity and predictability to areas that otherwise generate resentment. Tie your boundaries back to values and long term stability. "We are choosing not to take on more debt for your education than we can reasonably repay, because we do not want to be a financial burden on you later. That means we can contribute this amount; beyond that, we'll help you navigate scholarships, work, and school choices that fit."

When your teens push back (and they will) remember your longer term goal. You are not just trying to avoid conflict this month; you are trying to send a young adult into the world who understands that money choices have consequences, that opportunity is precious, and that they are capable of stewarding what they have. Each clear boundary, each debriefed mistake, each small win with saving or giving is one more brick in that foundation.

In the next chapter, we will zoom out from the day to day of raising kids to the broader question of generational wealth: how to transfer not only accounts and property, but also the mindset and systems that make those resources a blessing rather than a burden. For now, recognize that every time you teach your child to wait, to choose, to contribute, and to reflect, you are already doing that work. You are building stewards, not just spenders.

Chapter 14: Generational Wealth: Transfer the Money and the Mindset

Generational wealth is often pictured as a number: a portfolio balance, a business valuation, a real estate empire. But when you look at what actually lasts across decades, the pattern is very different. Money alone rarely survives two or three generations. What endures is a combination of assets, shared systems, and a clear sense of "this is who we are and what money is for." This chapter is about that fuller definition of generational wealth. You'll see why inheritances so often evaporate, how to articulate a family mission that ties your plan together, and how to build a "stewardship team" of heirs and helpers who can continue the work you've started.

You do not need to think of your family as "rich" for this to matter. If you have dependents, accounts, and a desire to leave something behind; whether that something is a paid-off house, a modest investment account, or a pattern of giving, then you are already doing legacy work. The question is whether the next generation will be equipped to receive it, manage it, and pass it further, or whether it will disappear into confusion, conflict, or lifestyle inflation. Let's start by looking clearly at why inheritances so often fail to do what parents hope they will.

Why Inheritances Often Disappear

Most family wealth doesn't last. A long-running study by the Williams Group found that roughly 70% of wealthy families lose their wealth by the second generation, and 90% by the third. The dominant causes are not tax law or market crashes; they are lack of preparation, poor communication, and unstructured transfers. Understanding those failure points gives you a checklist of what to do differently.

The first mistake is assuming that more money automatically creates more security. In practice, lack of skills (not lack of money) is what erodes even large inheritances. Heirs without basic financial literacy tend to overspend, make undisciplined investment choices, and are more vulnerable to scams and "can't-miss" opportunities. Some begin acting as if the inheritance has already arrived, taking on debt with an unspoken plan to "fix it later" when the estate is settled. That plan rests on assumptions that may not hold. The older generation might live longer than expected and spend more. Market downturns or poor investment decisions can shrink the estate. Charitable giving may redirect assets away from heirs. Even when a significant inheritance does arrive, a sudden windfall in the hands of someone who has never had to budget, invest, or say no is often more destabilizing than helpful. The antidote is gradual, age-appropriate responsibility that teaches kids and young adults how to manage small amounts well before they ever touch large sums.

A second, equally powerful force is silence. When parents avoid talking about money, estate intentions, or roles, they often believe they are "protecting" their children from worry or entitlement. In reality, secrecy creates a vacuum quickly filled with assumptions, rumors, and resentment. Siblings speculate about "who is getting what." Adult children are blindsided by decisions about executors, guardians, or business succession. Even when the ultimate distributions are fair, the process can feel like a betrayal because expectations were never aligned. The goal is not to share every account balance. It is to offer basic transparency: why you've made the choices you have, who is responsible for what, and where key documents live. When heirs understand the reasoning, they are far more likely to respect the structure rather than fighting it.

Timing and structure are the third failure point. Unstructured transfers at the wrong time—usually "everything at 18" or "whenever I die"—hand significant resources to people who may not yet have the maturity, habits, or stability to manage them. The gap in judgment between 18, 25, and 35 is enormous. Sudden access to large sums tends to amplify whatever patterns already exist. A disciplined young adult may use an inheritance to pay off high-interest debt, build a cushion, or invest for the long term. Someone with impulsive spending habits, addictions, or unstable relationships may burn through the same amount in a few years and be worse off than before. This is why many families structure staged distributions or milestone-based support: funds become available at defined ages or for documented purposes such as education, buying a first home, or starting a business. Trusts are another way to pass down wealth while encouraging good decision-making. For example, a trust might allow distributions for specific milestones such as education, home ownership, or business investments, but prevent unchecked spending that will deplete assets. Integrating mentorship into long-term planning creates space for heirs to learn from small mistakes and build confidence before stepping into larger roles.

Finally, many families have no continuity plan if one spouse dies or becomes incapacitated. It's common for one partner to "handle the money" and the other to vaguely trust that "it's all taken care of." But when the financially literate spouse is suddenly gone or unavailable, the survivor faces an immediate learning curve under maximum emotional stress. Bills, tax filings, business decisions, and beneficiary claims still need to be handled. Without updated beneficiaries, clear account access, and some sort of written continuity guide, critical assets can be delayed or misdirected. The operating system you've built so far in this book is your defense: a dashboard, emergency and estate binder, and shared knowledge. In the context of generational wealth, this is not just administrative housekeeping; it is the bridge that connects your planning to your spouse's ability to carry it forward.

Up to this point we've focused on what goes wrong. The rest of the chapter turns toward what you can build: a family wealth mission, and a team of prepared people who can execute it.

Your Family Wealth Mission Statement

Every durable enterprise, from a company to a charity, has some version of a mission: a short, clear statement that defines what resources are for and how decisions should be made. Families are no different. Without a mission, each generation improvises. With a mission, even imperfect future decisions can remain aligned with your core intent. Your first step is to articulate that intent together.

Begin with a values inventory as a couple. Set aside time and ask, "What do we want our money to do and not do for this family?" Brainstorm five to seven values that show up repeatedly in your choices: stability, education, generosity, entrepreneurship, service, faith, adventure, or something else. For each value, define what it looks like in daily life. If generosity is central, that might mean tithing, regular charitable giving, or helping extended family in structured ways. If stability is key, it might mean never carrying high-interest debt and maintaining robust emergency reserves. Just as important, name what you are willing to say no to in order to protect these priorities. Maybe that is a smaller house, fewer luxury trips, or choosing lower-cost colleges. As your children get older, you can invite their input in age-appropriate ways: "When you think about what kind of family we want to be, what words come to mind?"

From this raw material, craft a concise "Money is for..." statement. This is not marketing copy; it's a functional decision tool. A simple example might be: "In our family, money is for stability, opportunities to learn and grow, and generosity to others." Another might add "and time together" or "and the freedom to choose work we find meaningful." Once you have this sentence, translate it into concrete priorities: stability means cash reserves and insurance; opportunities to learn and grow mean funding education and experiences; generosity means a planned giving budget. Write this statement at the top of your family dashboard and in your emergency and estate binder so when hard trade-offs arise which could include having to choose between a bigger house and higher retirement contributions, or paying for an expensive school versus building a college fund, you can ask, "Which option better reflects what we said money is for?"

Consider writing a "legacy letter" to your kids as a companion to the technical documents in your estate plan. A legacy letter is a plain-language document that explains your story, your values, the lessons you learned about money and life, and your hopes for how your children will use what they inherit. It can also clarify expectations around responsibility, work ethic, and generosity: "We do not expect you to live off this money. We hope you will see it as a tool to support meaningful work, strong families, and service to others." This letter has no legal force, but it has significant emotional and relational power. Store it with your will and trust documents, and revisit it every few years as your perspective matures.

The final piece is to make your mission a living part of your system through an annual renewal ritual. During your yearly family wealth reset (described in the next chapter), read your mission statement aloud. Ask: Does this still fit our season of life? Have new responsibilities, like caring for aging parents shifted how we think about "what money is for"? Update language if needed, and then identify one concrete action for the coming year that visibly expresses the mission: increasing your giving percentage, funding a family scholarship, starting a small donor-advised fund, or simplifying your portfolio to reduce risk. This rhythm reinforces your identity as a steward family rather than a consumer family, and it anchors the numbers to a larger story.

Values and mission provide direction, but they do not execute themselves. For that, you need people: heirs, trustees, executors, guardians, and advisors who understand their roles and are prepared to fill them.

Heirs, Helpers, and Roles: Build the Stewardship Team

Generational wealth is not a solo project. By design, it outlives the people who initiate it. That means your operating system must include a "team" who can act on your behalf and eventually lead without you. Building this team is both a technical and relational task.

Start by clarifying the key roles and choosing the right people for each. An executor (or personal representative) settles your estate: gathering assets, paying debts, and following your will's instructions. This role calls for someone organized, steady under pressure, and able to communicate with multiple parties, not necessarily the oldest child. A guardian for minor children is primarily about parenting: who shares your values, can provide a stable home, and is genuinely willing to take on the responsibility? A trustee manages assets held in trust according to your instructions; this may require more financial competence and availability over time. Sometimes one person can fill multiple roles, but they do not have to. In fact, separating roles can reduce conflict. For example, having one sibling serve as guardian and another, or a professional, serve as trustee. The essential step is to ask people directly and respectfully, explain why you chose them, and confirm their willingness rather than assuming.

Gradually preparing heirs is a must. Think in phases. Phase 1, often in the teen years, is basic money management: budgeting, saving, understanding paychecks, and using a debit or starter credit card responsibly. Phase 2, typically in young adulthood, adds investing literacy and exposure to the family's financial structure: what accounts exist, the basics of your estate plan, and how to read a simple investment statement. Phase 3, as they demonstrate maturity, introduces higher-level stewardship: charitable planning, business governance, or co-trustee responsibilities. Along the way, create small "managed money" experiences. You might allocate a modest annual giving budget that your young adult researches and recommends recipients for, with you as a sounding board. Or you might let an adult child manage a small investment account within agreed guidelines, debriefing gains and losses together. These controlled experiences build judgment far more effectively than theoretical lectures.

Clarity is also your best tool for avoiding unequal outcomes that fracture families. Parents often wrestle with questions of fairness when children have different needs: one has a chronic illness, another chose a lower-paying but meaningful career, another received more support earlier in life. There is no one right formula, but there is a right process. Start by distinguishing equal from equitable. Equal might mean each child receives the same percentage of assets. Equitable might mean adjusting for specific situations, such as setting up a supplemental needs trust for a disabled child or leaving business interests to the child actually working in the business while equalizing others with different assets. Whatever you decide, document your reasoning clearly in your estate plan and, when appropriate, in your legacy letter. When adult children understand that differences reflect thoughtful consideration rather than favoritism or punishment, they are less likely to interpret them as rejection and more likely to respect the structure.

Philanthropy can be a powerful training ground for stewardship. Setting aside a defined portion of your budget or assets for giving allows the family to practice shared decision-making about money in a lower-stakes context. You might hold an annual "family giving meeting" where you review organizations or causes, listen to each member's proposal, and decide together how to allocate funds. Younger children can participate by choosing a local cause; teens can research charities' effectiveness; adult children might serve on the board of a family foundation or help administer a donor-advised fund. This process reinforces the idea that wealth carries responsibility, not just privileges, and that decisions should be anchored in values, not impulses. It also mirrors the kind of structured, communicative governance that helps families preserve wealth across generations.

Done well, the mission, roles, staged preparation, and shared giving, transform inheritance from a single event into an ongoing apprenticeship. You are not merely handing over accounts; you are inviting your heirs and helpers into a long-running project of stewardship. In the final chapter, you will see how to keep this entire operating system running through different life stages and major transitions, so that what you have built remains coherent, adaptable, and, most importantly, usable by the people you love.

Chapter 15: Keep It Running: Life-Stage Updates and the Annual Reset

A strong family wealth plan doesn't succeed because you made perfect decisions one January afternoon. It succeeds because you built something simple enough to revisit, again and again, as life changes. In that sense, the system you've created is less like a carved-in-stone monument and more like a living operating manual for your household. This chapter is about what it takes to keep that manual current: the yearly reset where you scan the whole system, the adjustments you'll make as you move through life stages, and the deliberate simplifications that allow the plan to survive your busiest, most stressful seasons.

The goal is not constant tinkering. The goal is a light, repeatable rhythm which serves as an annual reset plus a few smaller check-ins that keeps you from drifting for five or ten years without noticing that your insurance is outdated, your investing no longer matches your goals, or your estate plan doesn't match your current family structure. Thinking in cycles also aligns with how financial economists understand a household's "lifecycle" decisions: over time you smooth consumption, address changing risks, and reallocate resources as you move from building to preserving to spending down wealth. You don't need the math behind that to reap the benefit. You just need a calendar, your dashboard, and a couple of hours once a year.

The Annual Family Wealth Reset

Think of the annual reset as your household's "board meeting." Once a year, you and your partner step back from daily bills and emails and look at the entire operating system: cash flow, protection, investing, taxes, and legacy. The purpose is not to become analysts, but to make sure your real life and your written plan still match. To keep this review efficient and manageable, you'll do some preparation, follow a simple agenda, commit to one main improvement, and then deliberately acknowledge the progress you've made.

The reset begins before the meeting. A few days in advance, one of you triggers the pre-work checklist. You update your one-page dashboard: balances across checking, savings, investments, and debts; key insurance coverages; and your current monthly "burn rate." You pull declarations pages for home, auto, umbrella, and other property/liability coverage, plus summaries of life and disability insurance. Finally, you jot down major life changes since the last reset. Include job moves, children, health developments, relocations and a short list of the big goals you see over the next twelve months: perhaps paying off a specific loan, funding a home project, redoing estate documents, or hitting a contribution target. The aim is not exhaustive documentation; it's to make sure that when you sit down together, you're looking at the same, current snapshot.

When you actually sit down, your agenda follows the sequence used throughout this book: foundation, protection, growth, and legacy. First, you review your cash-flow framework: are your fixed, flex, and future-cost buckets realistic? Has your emergency fund stayed at or above target tiers, or have withdrawals or lifestyle creep eroded it? Where are you on your debt strategy, have balances moved the way your snowball or avalanche plan anticipated?

Next, you move to protection: you scan life and disability coverage amounts, beneficiary designations, estate documents, your emergency binder, and property and liability coverages. Have any life events created new needs, like a teen driver, a new mortgage, or a business side hustle?

Third, you revisit your investing and tax strategy: does your Investment Policy Statement still reflect your risk tolerance and timelines? Are contribution rates to retirement, HSAs, and education accounts on track relative to your targets? Do you need to plan tax actions for the year ahead, such as adjusting withholding or capturing additional deductions?

Finally, you look at legacy: guardianship designations, any trusts, your family mission statement, and your children's growing financial responsibilities. This sequence is designed to prevent blind spots. You are less likely to obsess about an extra 0.5% of investment return while ignoring a gaping disability coverage hole when you walk methodically through each layer.

The biggest trap in an annual reset is trying to fix everything at once. That's why you adopt the One-Decision Rule. After your review, you ask: "Of all the issues we just saw, which single improvement would create the most stability, clarity, or progress this year?" Maybe it's executing a trust, increasing retirement contributions by 3%, or buying an umbrella policy. You then translate that one decision into a 90-day action plan: specific steps, who owns each, and target dates. Everything else goes on a "later this year" list you can revisit at quarterly check-ins. Without this discipline, annual reviews turn into demoralizing marathons with a notebook of unresolved tasks and no clear priority.

You end the reset by reinforcing identity and progress. You look back over the year and name wins: a credit card paid off, an emergency fund tier reached, updated beneficiaries, a new monthly dashboard review habit. This is not a feel-good extra. Many beliefs and emotions about money are shaped by silence, family expectations, and a system that can feel rigged; no wonder many people find it exhausting to save or to understand investing. Consciously acknowledging progress helps rewrite that script. You re-read your family wealth mission statement, making any edits that reflect your current season. Then you mark the occasion with something simple but tangible like a favorite dessert, a walk, a small family outing. You are teaching yourselves and your kids: "We are the kind of family that leads our money together."

This annual rhythm stays consistent. What changes is which issues dominate the agenda as you move through life stages.

Life-Stage Playbooks: What Changes and What Stays

Your annual reset gives you a stable rhythm. But what you emphasize in those meetings will change as you move through different stages. A couple with toddlers and new mortgages faces different constraints than a couple in their late 50s with independent children. The operating system of your dashboard, meetings, funding order, IPS, estate basics stays constant. The dials you turn within that system shift.

In the young family, high cash-demand years, you are climbing a steep hill of expenses: childcare, housing upgrades, maybe a single income or a career break. Here the playbook is dominated by resilience basics. You prioritize building and preserving an emergency fund, even if you only reach the first tier at first. You make sure core insurance whether its term life, disability, or health, covers genuine worst cases. You tighten cash-flow automation: bills and savings first, then flexible spending, to prevent accidental overdrafts on already-tight months. Investing is intentionally simple: broad, diversified funds in tax-advantaged accounts, with contribution changes infrequent. Estate priorities are guardianship documents, powers of attorney, and beneficiary audits. You are not trying to optimize everything; you are trying to avoid catastrophic fragility while life is intense.

By mid-career, incomes often rise, but so does complexity: multiple accounts from job changes, stock compensation, older kids with emerging needs, aging parents, and perhaps side income or business interests. In this stage, optimization has a larger payoff. You deliberately increase retirement contributions to make use of peak earning years, potentially pushing toward or beyond employer-plan maximums. You sharpen your tax strategy: Roth vs. traditional allocations, HSA funding if eligible, and more disciplined year-end planning. Risk management gets a second look: do you now need umbrella coverage? Is your disability insurance still adequate? Does your estate plan need to incorporate trusts or more explicit instructions for teens?

You also fold teen-related planning into your agenda: clear college funding limits, plans for car costs, and age-appropriate responsibility training around earnings and spending. Here, the danger is not under-planning so much as spreading yourself thin; your operating system protects you from chasing every opportunity at the expense of core protections.

As you enter the pre-retirement years, the emphasis shifts from pure accumulation to risk reduction and clarity. The questions become: "Are we on track for enough?" and "How will cash flow work when paychecks stop?" You use your annual reset to clarify a retirement income concept. Consider roughly what will come from Social Security, what from portfolios, what from any pensions or rental properties. You reduce major unknowns by simplifying account structures and consolidating where appropriate, so that withdrawals a decade from now are straightforward. You reassess insurance: life insurance needs may decline; long-term disability may be less critical, but health coverage and possibly long-term care considerations become more salient. You finalize legacy structures which will include your trusts, updated wills, and clear beneficiary designations. Invest time in preparing heirs, not just documents. The operating system remains; your focus pivots from "grow as much as possible" toward "protect sufficiency and make it usable."

Not all stage changes are gradual. Sometimes your household is jolted into a new reality: a job loss, a serious diagnosis, divorce, the death of a spouse, or an unexpected relocation. In those moments, you reach for the recovery protocol. Step one is to stabilize cash flow: you revisit emergency fund tiers, cut or defer discretionary spending, and, if necessary, renegotiate payments or seek short-term assistance. Step two is communication. You increase the cadence of shorter money meetings. Weekly meetings for a period may be period, with an emphasis towards documenting every significant decision in your family money notes. This reduces cognitive and emotional load when you're under stress. Step three is restraint: you avoid major, irreversible financial moves (like taking on large new debts, liquidating retirement accounts, or making big investment bets) until your situation is clearer, unless safety or legal deadlines require action. The reset, in this context, is less about optimization and more about triage and preservation.

Across all of these stages, the pattern is consistent: major life events change your optimal choices, but they don't change the need for an integrated approach. Your household operating system gives you a way to absorb those shocks intentionally rather than reactively.

Simplify to Sustain: Less Complexity, More Consistency

As families earn more, save more, and invest more, a new threat emerges: complexity. Multiple old 401(k)s, overlapping bank accounts, tangled insurance policies, half-implemented side businesses, or a thicket of passwords. These don't just create friction; they increase the odds that something important will be forgotten or misaligned. Simplification is not about minimalism for its own sake. It is about engineering a system that continues to function when you are tired, distracted, or dealing with a crisis.

The first lever is consolidating where it genuinely helps. During an annual reset, you identify duplicate or low-value accounts: the dormant savings account opened for a promotion, the old employer plan you've meant to roll over, the small brokerage account with one position.

Where consolidating reduces maintenance and error risk without sacrificing meaningful benefits, you take action. At the same time, you maintain purposeful separation: a distinct bills account, a separate emergency fund, clearly labelled investment accounts. You then update your dashboard to reflect the new structure, so anyone reading it can understand the flow of money through your household at a glance.

The second lever is automating the "big rocks." Your operating system assumes willpower is limited and routes around it. Core retirement contributions are automated at the payroll level wherever possible; your emergency fund receives scheduled transfers until it hits your target tier, at which point those dollars are deliberately redirected to the next priority (debt payoff, college, taxable investing). Extra payments toward your highest-priority debts happen automatically after each payday. College or education contributions are automated too—but only after you've met a clearly defined minimum for retirement, so that you avoid sacrificing your own long-term stability out of short-term guilt. The less you have to remember, the more likely the plan is to endure.

The third lever is limiting your "decision surface area" which will be the number of choices you confront each month. You adopt default rules in advance: purchases above a set dollar amount trigger a 24-hour pause and a joint discussion; each raise automatically increases savings by a set percentage; you rebalance investments annually unless allocations drift outside pre-set bands. Your Investment Policy Statement becomes a shield against headline-driven changes: you have already decided under what conditions you will change asset allocation (life stage shifts, goal changes), so a volatile week in the markets does not require a fresh, emotional debate. You create a short list of "approved actions" for busy months: things you can do for your finances in 15 minutes or less, updating a beneficiary, increasing a contribution by 1%, or cancelling an unused subscription so that progress continues even when capacity is low.

The final lever is teaching the system as you live it, which converts maintenance into legacy. You let your children see the edges of the operating system: the monthly dashboard review, the annual reset, the way you talk about trade-offs. When they are young, this might simply be explaining that "every month, we decide together how to use our money so we can pay for today and save for the future." As they grow, you share specific elements: how you separate bills from fun spending, why you keep an emergency fund, how you chose your retirement savings targets. You do not burden them with adult anxieties; you model that money is a tool that can be directed intentionally. They will still make their own mistakes. But they will have seen what a functional, repeatable household wealth system looks like in practice.

Keeping your family wealth operating system running is not about constant vigilance. It is about a few well-chosen, well-protected rituals: an annual reset, occasional life-stage recalibrations, and ongoing simplification. If you keep those in place, your plan can adapt with you. From the chaos of raising small children to the decisions of pre-retirement and beyond you'll be more prepared and less likely to return to the fragile, reactive state you started from.

Conclusion

By now, you've done something most households never do: you've stopped treating money as a stream of chores and crises, and started treating it as something you lead. You've moved from reacting and opening apps only when a problem pops up, arguing when a bill surprises you to running a simple operating system for your family's wealth. The details of your life will keep shifting, but that shift in posture is permanent. You are no longer hoping that scattered good habits will add up to security. You're running a coherent plan, on purpose, together.

You can think of that plan as a single, four-part mental model. First is your foundation: the dashboard, cash-flow rails, emergency reserves, and debt strategy that keep the month-to-month stable. Second is protection: the insurance, estate documents, and liability and cyber safeguards that defend your income, your decisions, and the people who rely on you. Third is growth: the investing, tax decisions, retirement planning, real estate choices, and income strategy that turn today's effort into tomorrow's options. Fourth is legacy: how you teach your kids, structure inheritances, clarify your family mission, and prepare the next generation to steward what you've built. When you feel overwhelmed in the future, you don't need 50 tips; you need to ask, "Is this a foundation issue, a protection issue, a growth issue, or a legacy issue?" Then you know where to look and what kind of fix to make.

What makes this work in a real household is not more discipline. It is structure. The dashboard you built is your one-page reality check with the antidote to hand-waving about "how we're doing." The two-account cash-flow setup and your fixed–flex–future buckets mean bills and goals get covered before lifestyle expands. Your monthly 20-minute review, your 30-minute finance meeting, and your annual reset give you a predictable place to talk, decide, and adjust. Checklists like the emergency fund tiers, the insurance and estate binder, the tax and protection audits, mean you don't have to remember everything or reinvent it from scratch. Automation carries the weight: transfers to savings and investing, automatic debt paydowns, raise-capture rules, and scheduled contributions to education and giving. These systems turn good intentions into default behavior, so your family's wealth grows even when you're exhausted or distracted.

Along the way, you've almost certainly created concrete wins. Even if they felt small at the time. You've clarified what truly has to be paid every month and what can flex, and many of you have separated a bills account from a spending account for the first time. You've chosen a starter emergency buffer, maybe your first full month of essential expenses sitting in an account labelled for emergencies only, and for some of you, you've mapped out a full Tier 2 reserve. You've identified at least one money leak and plugged it, turning a forgotten subscription or bloated bill into deliberate progress. You've likely updated beneficiaries who had been wrong for years, increased life or disability coverage where it mattered, and written down who would do what in a genuine crisis. You've chosen a debt strategy on purpose, and you've stopped treating credit cards as a fallback plan.

You've also pushed into areas most couples avoid. Many of you have put in place the estate basics you'd kept on the mental to-do list for a decade such as wills, powers of attorney, guardianship choices, medical directives and organized them into a binder or digital vault that another adult could actually use. You've made tax-advantaged accounts part of an order of operations instead of a fog of acronyms, and you've written a simple Investment Policy Statement instead of chasing whatever the market is shouting about this month. You've named a realistic retirement target in ranges, not fantasies; run a basic gap analysis; and chosen at least one lever to move. You've set education support standards you can explain to your kids, rather than promising "we'll figure it out" at the last minute.

Most important, you've changed how you talk about money. Instead of fighting only when something goes wrong, you've created a standing place to talk when nothing is on fire. You've named your different money stories, recognized that safety and freedom are both valid priorities, and begun to translate them into shared rules instead of unspoken resentment. You've set thresholds for when you'll consult each other, carved out personal "no-questions-asked" spending, and started to treat transparency as a form of care, not control. The tone in your home around money may still be imperfect, but it is now anchored in structure and respect instead of in fear and avoidance.

None of this will insulate you from change. Jobs will shift, kids' needs will spike, parents will age, markets will move, and some years will simply be harder than others. The point is not to lock in a perfect plan and defend it forever. The point is to stay inside the system. When you're tired, you may not optimize investments, but you can keep the emergency fund separate and the basic automations on. When a disruption hits, you may not love every trade-off, but you have a dashboard, a binder, and a default agenda for a conversation that doesn't start in panic. When your life stage changes like a new child, new business, approaching retirement, you have a skeleton to update instead of a blank page to fill from scratch. Imperfect execution inside a solid framework will always beat heroic spurts followed by long stretches of neglect.

Going forward, both as a couple and as parents see yourselves as joint leaders of this system. The two of you are not just "bill payers" or "investors." You are the people who decide how this household absorbs shocks, creates stability, and opens doors for the next generation. Leading together means shared visibility and shared agency: no mystery accounts, no partner left in the dark, no one person silently carrying all the burden. As parents, your leadership shows up in what your kids see: that adults talk about trade-offs, plan for the future, protect each other, give on purpose, and sometimes say no now so they can say yes later. Whether you leave behind a modest nest egg or a substantial one, the culture you build around money will be the longest-lasting part of your legacy.

To keep your momentum, give yourselves a 30-day runway. In the first week, schedule one dashboard session: gather your accounts, update your one-page view, and agree on who owns keeping it current. In the second week, choose one protection review: confirm life and disability coverage, verify beneficiaries, or walk through your emergency and estate binder together and fill one obvious gap. In the third week, implement one automation upgrade: increase a retirement or HSA contribution by even 1–2%, turn on automatic transfers to your emergency fund or education account, or auto-route a portion of your next raise using your own raise-capture rule. In the fourth week, hold one short family meeting: review the month's decisions with your spouse, revisit your "money is for..." statement, and, if your kids are old enough, invite them into a small part of the plan allowing them to be apart of a giving choice, a savings goal, or a conversation about an upcoming expense. Four simple moves, one per week, will turn this conclusion into continued motion.

Finally, don't try to do this in total isolation. Share the high-level version of your plan with at least one other person or couple you trust. That might be a sibling, a close friend, a mentor, or a professional advisor. Tell them, in your own words, how you've structured your foundation, protection, growth, and legacy. Articulating it out loud will sharpen your thinking; inviting questions will expose weak spots gently, before life does it brutally. If you find an advisor who respects your time and your values, use them as a thinking partner, not a driver of your decisions. And within your own walls, keep bringing your children further into the story as they mature. The more your household treats money as something you steward together, practicing transparency, discussion, and alignment with your mission, the less power, fear and confusion will have. You have built an operating system designed for real families, in real life. Now your work is simply to keep using it, one decision, one meeting, and one season at a time.

Reference List

40 Tex. Admin. Code § 700.526 - What is Tier II: Complex Mental Health Services to Support Stabilization Package? (2024). LII / Legal Information Institute. https://www.law.cornell.edu/regulations/texas/40-Tex-Admin-Code-SS-700-526

Active vs. Passive Investing. (2025, May 20). Finra.org. https://www.finra.org/investors/insights/active-passive-investing

Bank, T. S. (2025, December 16). *An Age-By-Age Guide to Teaching Kids About Money - Southern Bank.* Southern Bank. https://thesouthern.bank/blog/an-age-by-age-guide-to-teaching-kids-about-money/

Broderick, L. (2025, May 21). *Navigating Financial Planning with a Reluctant Partner: 5 Tips for Success - Bankers Life Blog*. Bankers Life Blog. https://www.bankerslife.com/insights/personal-finance/navigating-financial-planning-with-a-reluctant-partner-5-tips-for-success/

Bank, J. S. (2024, December 12). *Buying Below Your Means: The Case for a Smaller Home.* Jsb.bank; Jefferson Security Bank. https://www.jsb.bank/resources/buying-below-your-means-the-case-for-a-smaller-home

Emergency fund: Why you need one | Vanguard. (n.d.). Investor.vanguard.com. https://investor.vanguard.com/investor-resources-education/emergency-fund

English, R. (2024, November 19). *Preparing Heirs for Inheritance: Financial Literacy & Estate Planning*. Commercetrustcompany.com; Commerce Trust. https://www.commercetrustcompany.com/research-and-insights/articles/estate-planning-for-high-net-worth-families-preparing-heirs-for-an-inheritance

Educating the Next Generation in Wealth Stewardship. (2025, November 5). MGO CPA. https://www.mgocpa.com/perspective/educating-next-generation-wealth-stewardship/

Family banking: A simple guide to benefits and strategies. (2025, April 15). Associatedbank.com; Associated Bank. https://www.associatedbank.com/education/articles/personal-finance/banking-basics/family-banking-benefits-and-strategies

Financial Planning Through Life Stages | U.S. Bank. (2020, November 20). Usbank.com. https://www.usbank.com/wealth-management/private-wealth-management/financial-planning-through-life-stages.html

Free Planning Tools - My Fed University - Retirement Planning Tools. (2025, May 19). My Fed University. https://myfeduniversity.com/free-planning-tools/

How to Ask for a Promotion and Level Up in Your Career. (2025). Indeed Career Guide. https://www.indeed.com/career-advice/pay-salary/negotiate-promotion-salary

Kagan, J. (2021, September 30). *What Is the Needs Approach?* Investopedia. https://www.investopedia.com/terms/n/needsapproach.asp

Living Trust vs. Will: Key Differences & Which to Choose. (2025). MetLife. https://www.metlife.com/stories/legal/living-trust-vs-will/

Life Insurance Needs Calculator. (n.d.). Life Happens. https://lifehappens.org/life-insurance-needs-calculator/

Personal Umbrella Insurance Policy (PUP) | Allstate. (2023). Allstate. https://www.allstate.com/personal-umbrella-policy

Patek, A. (2025, November 19). *Allowance And Chores: For Learning Or Earning?* Generation Mindful. https://genmindful.com/blogs/mindful-moments/allowance-and-chores-for-learning-or-earning?srsltid=AfmBOoqKXepZCyGkxxTpwfArdXBrNfm6n0L8TtT8_eb7qbTDpatWgkx2

Paxton, K. (2023). *Help Prevent Identity Theft | Office of the Attorney General.* Www.texasattorneygeneral.gov. https://www.texasattorneygeneral.gov/consumer-protection/identity-theft/help-prevent-identity-theft

Ramsey Solutions. (2026, February 23). *Side Hustles for Parents: How to Earn Extra Money (Without Leaving Home).* Ramsey Solutions. https://www.ramseysolutions.com/saving/Side-Hustles-for-Parents-How-to-Earn-Extra-Money-Without-Leaving-Home?srsltid=AfmBOorXBx1rO3u9iAIstsV_NXmA8rwmhJ97ChZkJIIarIo-ndSzbU4J

Real Estate Risk Management: Strategies to Protect Investment. (2024, September 27). The Baldwin Group. https://baldwin.com/insights/real-estate-risk-management-strategies-to-protect-your-investments/

Steen, M. (2024, March 4). *Keys to creating a family investment policy statement*. Family Business Magazine. https://familybusinessmagazine.com/wealth-management/keys-to-creating-a-family-investment-policy-statement/

Sutton, T. (2025, December 4). *Year-End Tax Planning Strategies for High-Net-Worth Families*. Creative Planning. https://creativeplanning.com/insights/taxes/year-end-tax-planning-high-net-worth-families/

Smith, J. P., McArdle, J. J., & Willis, R. (2010, October 19). *Financial Decision Making and Cognition in a Family Context*. The Economic Journal. https://doi.org/10.1111/j.1468-0297.2010.02394.x

The ABCs of HSAs. (2026, January 8). Bairdwealth.com; RWBaird Wealth. https://www.bairdwealth.com/insights/wealth-management-perspectives/2021/12/the-abcs-of-hsas/

The Emergency Binder Checklist: Be Ready for Life's What-Ifs | USSFCU | Washington, D.C. - Alexandria VA - Bethesda, MD. (2025). Senate Cents: A Financial Wellness Blog. https://www.ussfcu.org/media-center/senate-cents-a-financial-wellness-blog/blog-detail.html?cId=96062&title=the-emergency-binder-checklist-be-ready-for-life-s-what-ifs

Welcome To Zscaler Directory Authentication. (2025). Loc.gov. https://guides.loc.gov/personal-finance/life-stages

Zaccardi, M. (2024, August 8). *Understanding a Retirement Gap Analysis*. SoFi. https://www.sofi.com/learn/content/retirement-gap-analysis/

admin. (2024, July 11). *7 Tips For Budgeting And Staying Focused On Your Goals | WVJC | October 2024*. WVJC. https://www.wvjc.edu/7-tips-for-budgeting-and-staying-focused-on-your-goals/

espeal. (2022, February 11). *Communication Strategies for Talking about Money with a Significant Other*. Onlinecounselingprograms.com. https://onlinecounselingprograms.com/resources/finance-issues-in-a-relationship/

Family Wealth Dashboard (Free)

Scan Me

Your Feedback

You just finished the Family Wealth Formula and your financial life is already starting to look different!

Please take 60 seconds to leave an honest review on Amazon. Your words help other families find the operating system they need and they mean more than you know.

Simply scan the code below with your phone's camera to share your thoughts

Scan Me

Other Books In This Series

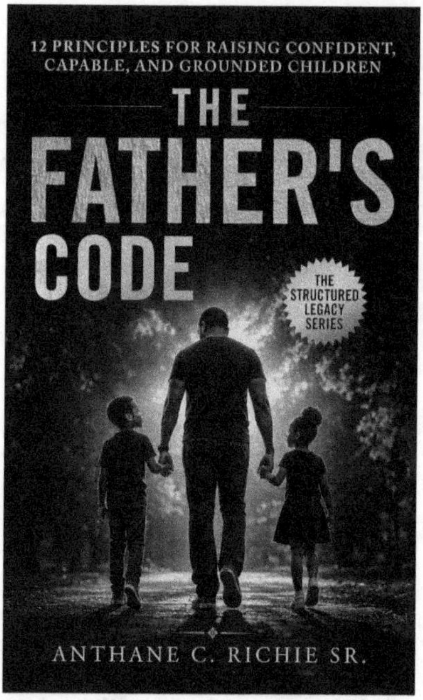

Building family wealth is only half the equation. The other half is the man leading the home.

The Father's Code is a practical field manual for the over-scheduled, growth-oriented dad who wants to lead his family with intention and not just provide for them. Built around 12 core codes, it gives you the tools to set the emotional temperature of your home, repair when you fail, and build a legacy your kids will carry into their own lives.

www.ingramcontent.com/pod-product-compliance
Lightning Source LLC
LaVergne TN
LVHW010724061126
851857LV00014B/1338